DARREL

FAITH

OR

FRUSTRATION

28 27 26 25 24 23 22   10 09 08 07 06 05 04

Faith or Frustration
ISBN-13: 978-0-89276-974-2
ISBN-10: 0-89276-974-2

Copyright © 1975 Rhema Bible Church
ᴀᴋᴀ Kenneth Hagin Ministries, Inc.
Printed in the USA

In the U.S. write:
Kenneth Hagin Ministries
P.O. Box 50126
Tulsa, OK 74150-0126
1-888-28-FAITH
rhema.org

In Canada write:
Kenneth Hagin Ministries of Canada
P.O. Box 335, Station D
Etobicoke (Toronto), Ontario
Canada M9A 4X3
1-866-70-RHEMA
rhemacanada.org

TABLE OF CONTENTS

■

ACKNOWLEDGEMENTS

I wish to thank Rev. Kenneth E. Hagin for introducing me to the life of faith. I am deeply indebted to him for the foundation of the word of faith he imparted to me.

I also want to thank Pastor Kenneth Hagin Jr. for the great encouragement he has given me to use my faith to fulfill my calling and ministry.

I appreciate all the work that Stephanie Pack did in making this manuscript possible.

Most of all, I want to thank my dear wife, Bonnie, for always being there for me. Together we have walked by faith and shall continue to do so.

■

INTRODUCTION

S ociety today is full of frustrated people. If you turn on the
television, you will see program after program trying to help
people solve their frustrations about their weight, relationships,
jobs, family, finances—and the list goes on. We Christians often fall
into that same category, allowing our problems to consume us. We
become dissatisfied and are quick to tell anyone who will listen just
how bad it *really* is.

God, on the other hand, operates in faith and demands that His
children do the same. In fact, faith is the law by which we are mea-
sured. Faith is an absolute. It is neither a suggestion, nor something
simply to ponder. It is an action.

HEBREWS 11:3, 6

3 Through faith we understand that the worlds were framed by the word
of God, so that things which are seen were not made of things that do
appear. . . .

6 But without faith it is impossible to please him: for he that cometh to God
must believe that he is, and that he is a rewarder of them that diligently
seek him.

Therefore, Christians must understand and walk in faith. Unfortunately, many of us have replaced faith with works. We look for the
newest three-step program that promises a supernatural change in

our circumstances. Instead of taking the necessary steps—faith and patience—to receive God's promises, we run around trying to find something that promises quick success (Heb. 6:12; 10:36).

In this hour, it is especially important that believers come back into the realm of faith. In fact, the entire Body of Christ must learn to walk in faith daily. Without faith, we cannot please God, nor can we do everything God has called us to do individually and corporately—the greatest of which is to be His ambassadors to a world that is lost and in need of a savior.

God's plans for us are good and they are definite. However, they become a reality only if we believe in Him and in His promises. The Lord has already declared His plans *"to prosper you and not to harm you, plans to give you hope and a future"* (Jer. 29:11 NIV). We can infer from this verse that our response to Him and to His Word is the determining factor of our success. Only by walking in faith can we fulfill everything He has promised and planned.

The Book of Hebrews tells of some faith heroes, commending them for their lifestyle. Their life of faith set them apart from everyone else around them (Heb. 11:2). Believers today need to be set apart as well. No matter what the circumstances, God's Word tells me that I must have confidence in God and in His promises if I am to be commended as the heroes of the Bible were. As a believer, I have that choice to make every day.

Now believers in the twenty-first century have very different dreams and goals than those of the Bible heroes of faith, but the principle for attaining them remains the same. It does not matter

■

Introduction

who you are or what you have been called to do. Whether you are a preacher or a miner, a teacher or a doctor, the path to success is still that of faith.

If you are to succeed in this lifestyle of faith, you must understand two important principles. These principles will keep you grounded when everything around you appears to be shifting and unpredictable.

First, you need to understand that faith is not tangible. You cannot touch it, or taste it. Neither can you comprehend faith with your mind. It is an inward force of the heart. The Apostle Paul actually spoke of "the spirit of faith" in a letter to the Church at Corinth (2 Cor. 4:13).

Second, your actions are to be based on your faith, not on your circumstances or feelings. The Bible says we are to walk by faith and not by sight (2 Cor. 5:7). Walking by faith simply means that you rely on the Lord all the time. In other words, you always trust who He is (His character and nature) and what He says (His promises). You do not turn faith on and off as your needs change. Faith is not just something we try to activate when we receive a bad report from our doctor, or when we are faced with unexpected bills. No, walking by faith should be the way we live 24 hours a day, 7 days a week, 52 weeks a year (Gal. 3:11).

Yet, many times we fail to "get in faith" until a problem must be solved. Instead of living by faith, most of us live in frustration. We move from crisis to crisis with differing measures of success from one time to another.

Although Galatians 3:11 affirms that *"the just shall live by faith,"* we sometimes think this is only achieved by ministers or those we call saints. That couldn't be further from the truth, for God has given the same measure of faith to every man (Rom. 12:3). Therefore, it is up to you and me to discover how we can learn to walk in faith.

■

A Word to You

Take the first step! I guarantee that you will not be disappointed. Your life of frustration can be permanently traded in for a life of faith.

What are you waiting for? Let's embark on this adventure of purpose together!‾

Hope—The Missing Ingredient

Faith operates in the unseen realm. It is a spiritual force that we can't see, taste, touch, hear, feel, or smell. So, we must find another way to know more about the subject.

In my search to know more about faith, the Holy Spirit began to speak to me about the importance of hope. He said, "Faith is motivated by your hope; frustration is motivated by your problems." He further said, "My people are in frustration; they are not in faith." I had never heard anyone teach it that way. In fact, I had to sit on it for a while and think about what He had told me. Then God said, "If you get consumed with hope, you will be in faith, [but] My people are so consumed with their problems that they are frustrated."

I answered, "Okay, but Lord, I need to see something here. What is this hope and faith?"

Looking at Hebrews 11:1, I saw that "faith is the substance of things hoped for, [and] the evidence of things not seen." Since that's the case, I must first understand what hope is if I ever want to be a person who operates in faith. The Lord then began to show me that without hope my faith has nothing to go after.

Hope is the missing ingredient. Without it, I won't make the finish line. Hope is what my faith is running to obtain. Hope is my goal, my vision and my dream; it is the revelation of what God said He would do for me. Faith, well-grounded in Bible hope, will go out to get whatever you need and bring it back to you. However, too many of us are trying to release faith when faith has nothing to go after.

For the sake of illustration, think about a well-trained dog. One of his favorite games is "fetch." If you toss a ball, he takes off. The dog will run to the toy, grab it, and bring it back to you; and he will do this over and over and over. Hours, days, or months may pass, but as soon as you let him know you are ready to throw, the dog comes!

Now think of it this way: The dog represents your faith (I call him "Faith Dog"), and the ball represents your hope. You need to take your hope (your dreams and God-given plans) and throw! Your faith then has something to go after. Don't be fooled, though. Faith will sit at your feet—just like a dog—until it has something to fetch. Faith cannot run after something that's not there!

Confident Expectation

Studying further, I found out that the Greek definition for hope is "a confident expectation."[1] So then, putting hope and faith together, I saw that faith is the substance of what I confidently expect God to do for me. Therefore, hope begins to give me something to expect. Without hope, I have nothing to release my faith for.

Let me tell you a story. It's one of hope. It's about me, and brownies.

Have you ever been out traveling on the road and gotten a hankering for something sweet? Well, I have. When I drive somewhere, nothing is better to keep me going than a good cup of coffee and a Little Debbie Chocolate Fudge Brownie. I don't mind the hours behind the wheel, or even the weather, because I know that eventually I'm going to round a corner and find a gas station. I have a confident expectation that when I park the car and walk into that store, I'm going to find exactly what I want!

Sometimes when I'm traveling on familiar roads, I'll even pass up a few gas stations and go five or ten miles farther just so I can get the kind of brownie I like. I don't worry because I know I will eventually get to the right store, if I just keep driving. My faith leads me, and before long, I'm sipping on a hot cup of coffee and popping a piece of fudge brownie into my mouth.

Think about this. If I never had an expectation (a goal)—such as the hope of biting into my favorite treat—I would have nothing to reach for. I would keep on driving, mile after mile. Isn't that like our lives sometimes? If we don't have something that we are confidently expecting (a God-given vision and plan in our heart), we really don't have anything for our faith to give substance to.

Sadly, many people today have no expectations. They just get up, go to work, return home, and then go to bed. Do you fall into that category? What are your expectations? What are you confidently expecting God to do for you?

Anticipation

One day, while continuing my studies, I discovered that the word hope also means "to anticipate something with pleasure." So, I began to think of faith as the substance of those things I was anticipating (with pleasure) that God would do for me. Hope, then, causes me to eagerly wait for God to bring my dreams and visions to pass.

As I thought about hope in this new way and looked at its importance, God showed me something. He said, "Hope is the Christmas present sitting under the tree a week before Christmas, and you're the kid with his name on the tag." Suddenly, I could see it!

Children wait for their parents to put gifts under the tree, and without thinking twice, they run over and start looking through the wrapped packages. They find the ones marked for them and then begin to pick up each package, thinking of the pleasure that's coming. Christmas may still be a week off, but they just can't wait. They have to try to figure out what's inside. (Talk about extreme pleasure—just look at their faces!) That's hope!

Those children are confident that Mom and Dad have bought them their secret desires and wishes. They just believe that everything from their Christmas list is sitting under that tree. In fact, the kids have already begun to plan how they're going to play with their new toys, and which of their friends they will invite over first for an afternoon of fun. If you could hear what they were thinking, it would sound something like this: "Mom and Dad got it! They must have seen those notes I left all over the house. I just know they bought it for me. After all, I took them to the store and showed them exactly what I want. And this box here is exactly the right size. Boy, . . . I can't wait till Christmas!"

With two days to go until Christmas, the energy level is almost more than anyone can stand. The children's excitement is contagious. The countdown continues and when Christmas morning rolls around, the children are more than ready to tear off that beautiful paper covering up their presents. That's hope!

As I thought about what God said, I saw something else: Faith opens the package of hope and receives the prize out of it. As a child, you hoped and you hoped and you hoped that the present under the tree was exactly what you were wanting. You had a confident expectation that Mom and Dad had gotten exactly what you wanted. So much so, that you kept looking at the package with anticipation, pleasure, and joy. And even though the wrapping paper made it look good, you opened it as quickly as you could . . . knowing that the gift inside was something far better than the package itself. Thank God for the hope that takes you to Christmas morning, but it's your faith that lets you open the gifts waiting for you.

What is your hope? What is your package? If your hope is healing, then begin to anticipate it with pleasure. See it sitting under the tree—the Cross of Christ. Expect to open it. Build your hope on the Word of God! Gain the confidence that God said it is yours. If your body is filled with pain, begin to anticipate with pleasure doing what everyone else can do with no pain, then confidently expect it to happen. Get so excited about it that you start to praise God. When you do, you'll begin to talk about your present. You'll tell anyone and everyone that God has healed you.

With your hope sitting under the tree, faith springs into action. Hope will draw you to your present. Then, your faith will get to the place that it can't wait any longer. It will reach down, pick up that box of healing, and rip it open. Hope is wonderful, but faith tears open the package!

Your presents are under the tree, under the Cross of Calvary. What are you waiting for? Build your hopes on the Word of God, and begin to look for God's gifts to you. When you find them, tear them open by faith, and receive what God has already bought for you!

That's Hope!

Some Christians may truly think they are in hope. They can see God's promises (His presents) all wrapped up and sitting under the tree. However, they never make it to Christmas morning. They never unwrap the gifts with their name on them.

I'd like to challenge you today to examine yourself. What does your conversation sound like? Are you excitedly telling everyone who comes your way about your package under the tree, or does your conversation sound a bit like this?

"How are you doing?"

"I'm just hanging on . . . but I think I'm going to make it . . . you all pray for me. I just don't understand it. I've made the right confessions.

I was even in the prayer line and had Pastor lay hands on me. I've felt the power of God, and I have spoken the Word. I was believing God, but I still have the problem."

If that's the way you talk, then you have no hope. No expectation is there, and no anticipation of pleasure—only confusion. Your frustration is talking, not faith. One thing is sure: you're not going to get anywhere talking like that. Instead, your conversation must reflect what you believe in your heart. It should give a glimpse of joyful and confident expectation, something like this:

"How are you doing?"

"Glory to God, I'll tell you how I'm doing. First Peter 2:24 says, 'by his stripes I was healed,' and I am anticipating a full manifestation. Hallelujah! In fact, all I've been doing is praising and thanking God, speaking His Word. I'm giving substance to it, and I'm getting better. I am not moved by what I see. I am not moved by what I feel. I don't perceive as real fact what my senses tell me. I am not going to forsake my mercy by being caught up in vanity. I am going to go ahead and keep my eyes on God. I'm telling you right now that God is going to heal me. Hallelujah!"

Now you have hope and faith working together. Now you are expecting your healing to come to pass. Now hope is motivating your faith. Now you are doing it God's way!

Others of us, if we would admit it, have no idea what to hope for. We have gotten stuck in a defensive position, yet almost all of us know that we can't win if we never go on the offense. Nevertheless, many of us haven't even taken the time to find out what God's hopes and desires are for us. We're too busy living from day to day.

You must begin to see beyond where you find yourself today. Why? Without vision, you will die, right in the middle of your problems (Prov. 29:18). So, look to the Word and find out what it has to say about you. Then, set goals for your life. When you begin to discover what God's vision (His hope) is for you, it will be easier to believe that God already has some presents for you to open—healing, prosperity, a home, a family, a job, wisdom, and favor—just to name a few.

"Okay, Brother Huffman," you may ask, "how am I going to get some hope?"

Well, I'll show you two ways you can begin to operate in hope. Either one will put you back in an offensive position and on your way to victory. You will find the first one in the Book of Ephesians. The Apostle Paul is writing to every believer:

EPHESIANS 1:16–18

16 [I] cease not to give thanks for you, making mention of you in my prayers;

17 That the God of our Lord Jesus Christ, the Father of glory, may give unto you the spirit of wisdom and revelation in the knowledge of him:

18 The eyes of your understanding being enlightened; that ye may know what is the hope of his calling . . . .

You can see that you must first ask God to show you what to hope for. Ask Him to lead you to what He wants for you. Ask Him to show you what He wants you to do (Rom. 8:14). If you ask, He will give you a revelation of what you should be hoping for. How will that happen? Look at the following scriptures:

ROMANS 8:14

14 For as many as are led by the Spirit of God, they are the sons of God.

JAMES 1:5

5 If any of you lack wisdom, let him ask of God, that giveth to all men liberally, and upbraideth not; and it shall be given him.

The Lord has promised that His children will be led by His Spirit. So, open your heart and pray, "Lord, what do You want me to expect with anticipation and confidence? What do You want me to joyfully anticipate? God, what is Your hope for my life? Please, show me my hope, my goals, and my vision. Give me a revelation of Your will so I can use my faith for it. Make hope a reality in my life."

God's promises must become real to *you*. For example, you can't hope to get healed just because someone else said you should. You *should* be healed, but it will happen only when you begin to read God's Word and find out His will for you concerning healing.

Hope is the goal, the vision, the plan that God has ordained for you to walk out. Until you find it, you will have nothing for your faith to give substance to. This is true for every part of your life: prosperity, social and business success, family, and ministry.

So, if I want to give my faith something to go after, the first thing I need to do is to pray for God to deposit into my spirit His hope for me, "Father, I want You right now to reveal to me the hope that

I need to use my faith for. I am praying right now for the spirit of wisdom and revelation to open my spirit man and reveal the hope of what You called me to have.

"God, show me what I am to confidently expect. Show me what I am to anticipate with joy. Show me Your prophetic revelation for my life, so I can use my faith and bring it into reality. Lord, give me something that I can get up in the morning and want. Give me something that I can shout and pray about. Put Your hope for me in my heart so that I can begin to use my faith and bring it to pass. Then You can get glory from my life. Amen."

When you ask the Lord to show you what He desires for your life, hope will begin to grow and develop in your heart. How can you tell if you are in hope? It's simple.

Hope is much like anticipating a special event. The closer and closer you get to the day, butterflies begin to flutter around inside you. All the excitement makes you want to jump up and down. You can hardly stand the wait. You may even find yourself saying, "Man, I'm joyfully anticipating that God is going to bring this to pass for me!"

Psalm 37:4 tells us the second way to operate in hope. The *New International Version* says, "Delight yourself in the Lord, and he will give you the desires of your heart." It might help, however, if you think of it like this: Delight yourself in the Lord, and He will *place* His desires in your heart. (If you will study it in the Hebrew, you will find it reads that way.)

To delight yourself in the Lord means "to sing in the Spirit, to worship and praise God, and to pursue Him." When you spend time in His presence, He will place His hopes, His dreams, and His desires inside you. Actually, you simply become more and more like Him. His hope becomes your hope and His desires, your desires.

Remember, Hebrews 11:6 tells us, "He is the rewarder of those who earnestly and diligently seek Him [out]" (AMPC).

Joyful Rest

Now that you know how to get the hope you need, don't stop there. Add your faith to your hope. Remember that your ultimate goal is to *see* what you have been hoping for. Your faith is going to keep working and working until it can open that package of hope.

Faith will eventually give tangibility and reality to the hope in your heart. Knowing that will cause you to enter into rest. That's right! Rest comes when you are walking in faith toward your hope:

JOB 11:18
18 And thou shalt be secure, because there is hope; yea, thou shalt dig about thee, and thou shalt take thy rest in safety.

Someone may ask, "How can you have such rest?"

"I have hope in my heart."

"What do you mean you have hope?"

"I'm not talking about just *a hopin' and a prayin.'* [As we say in West Virginia!] I mean that I spent time with God, seeking Him, and by the spirit of wisdom and revelation I now see His desire (His hope) for me. Since I saw His plan, I am joyfully anticipating it coming to pass. In fact, I am now enjoying the trip toward its full manifestation just as much as I will when it manifests."

When you have hope working in your life, you can be joyful while you're waiting for the manifestation to come. You can have fun while you are being healed. You can have fun while you are becoming prosperous. You can have fun while you are waiting on the answer to your prayer. You can have fun while that loved one is still lost. All the while, you can be just shouting the victory!

God's Plan

Release your faith only after you have found out God's plan. Don't come up with your own plan and then present it to God. No! That's the dumbest thing you could do. Instead, go to God first, because He already has a plan.

The Apostle Paul told the Corinthians that God has already provided a way of escape from every temptation. That means God must have a plan for you. He has already designed a way to get you through whatever is happening to you right now. He promises a way of escape so you can bear up under the temptation, making it through to the victory side:

1 CORINTHIANS 10:13

13 There hath no temptation [test, trial, struggle or problem] taken you but such as is common to man: but God is faithful, who will not suffer you

to be tempted above that ye are able; but will with the temptation also make a way to escape, that ye may be able to bear it.

You can trust the Lord and have confidence in His hope for you. You can rely on Him with an inward certainty, right in the middle of any test that comes your way. If you do, the test will not consume you. You will not become frustrated when you know that you can trust the Lord. Rather, you will be walking in faith.

Before we go any further, I must remind you that this verse does not say that God brings the temptation. Many people falsely believe that the Lord brings temptations to their door. That is not true! It is true, however, that He will not allow you to be tempted above what you are able to bear (with His help). Remember, He is the One who makes a way for your escape.

JAMES 1:13
13 Let no man say when he is tempted, I am tempted of God: for God cannot be tempted with evil, neither tempteth he any man.

JAMES 1:13 (AMPC)
13 Let no one say when he is tempted, I am tempted from God; for God is incapable of being tempted by [what is] evil and He Himself tempts no one.

When you are in the middle of your test and don't know what to do, God does. Perhaps you feel as if you're in a maze, and you've lost all sense of direction. Don't worry! God will be your guide. He has the map that will show you how to get out, and once you know how to get out, you can use your faith and start walking to the exit. When you know where you are going, you can enjoy the journey.

You have no reason to sweat when you have the map and a guide! In fact, you can then use your map to help others out of the same maze.

If you can get hold of God's plan of escape, then all you have to do is follow it. Faith is simply following God's plan for you. Notice that I said faith is following *God's* plan, not someone else's plan. In other words, you will only reach your goals—obtain your hope by faith—by doing things God's way, not man's.

The devil may light a fire in order to create a smoke screen, but that won't matter. When you have your hope (your plan) and you're using your faith to bring your hope to pass, then you can walk right through the smoke. It won't stop you or slow you down because you have your Guide telling you exactly where to go and what to do.

You'll be just like the race car driver who drives through the smoke, avoiding the wreckage around him. He has someone on his team telling him which path to take. He can't see, but he puts the pedal to the metal because he has just been told the road is clear in front of him. He shoots through the smoke, missing bumpers and passing debris.

As you race toward your hope, it won't matter if the devil throws some smoke in your way because you have the Holy Spirit speaking in your ears. You will be able to keep the pedal of faith right down to the floorboard because the Lord has already made a way for you to get through that trouble. Everyone else may crash around you, but you will be able to cross the finish line without fear. Your hope will feed your faith. When that happens, your faith will make your hope a reality, and you will be the victor standing in the winner's circle.

■
_____

A WORD TO YOU

It is safe to say that if you are confidently expecting something and anticipating it with pleasure, you will not become frustrated waiting for it. Unfortunately, many of us have not understood this concept. Many of us today have lost our hope.

Perhaps you've let the devil come in and steal it, or perhaps you simply have forgotten the dreams and desires you once had but placed on the shelf long ago. Whatever the reason, you cannot walk in faith if you lose your hope.

Before you can go any further, you will need to evaluate where you are. To do that, answer these questions:

Do you have vision in your spirit that you are anticipating with pleasure?

If so, are you enjoying the trip along the way to your destination?

Do you have something burning on the inside of you?

Do you have a passion?

Do your priorities line up with your hope?

If you don't have a hope, or have forgotten or dropped it along the way, the answer to all of these questions would be "No."

If you have no hope, you're having a difficult time getting out of bed in the morning. Prayer and devotions have even become a struggle. Without hope, you are merely surviving or existing. Frustration has set in, and you're in trouble!

CHAPTER
TWO

Faith or Frustration—Where Are You?

Faith is reaching out to achieve what God called you to do; frustration is sitting around fussing about it. Faith causes you to speak the vision; frustration causes you to speak the problem. Hope is the source of your faith, while the problem is the source of your frustration. Therefore, faith and frustration are opposites; you can't be in faith and frustration at the same time.

Frustration's entire purpose is to prevent you from achieving your goal (your hope). The following definitions will help to make this plain:

Frustrate—1. to make (plans, efforts, etc.) worthless or of no avail; defeat; nullify. 2. to disappoint or thwart (a person).[1]

Frustration—1. act of frustrating; state of being frustrated. 2. something that frustrates, as an unresolved problem. 3. a feeling of dissatisfaction, often accompanied by anxiety or depression, resulting from unfulfilled needs or unresolved problems.[2]

So, where are you—faith or frustration? The answer to that question will be the tell-tale sign of your future success. Frustration will rob you; refuse to let it do so!

Instead, build and strengthen your hope by renewing your mind to what the Word of God says is yours. All the while, keep in mind that the devil knows the priority of the Word. Don't allow him to steal it from you. Don't let him take away the source of your hope, for your faith falters without hope.

In Mark chapter 4, Jesus told His disciples the parable of the sower. He explained that the devil immediately comes to steal the Word when it has been sown into the soil of our heart. In other words, the devil comes to steal the plan of God out of your life. He comes to afflict and persecute you by tossing distractions and the cares of this life into your path. If he can get you caught up in a struggle—if he can get you frustrated—he will succeed in stealing the Word of God upon which your hope is based.

MARK 4:14–19 (AMPC)

14 The sower sows the Word.

15 The ones along the path are those who have the Word sown [in their hearts], but when they hear, Satan comes at once and [by force] takes away the message which is sown in them.

16 And in the same way the ones sown upon stony ground are those who, when they hear the Word, at once receive and accept and welcome it with joy;

17 And they have no real root in themselves, and so they endure for a little while; then when trouble or persecution arises on account of the Word, they immediately are offended (become displeased, indignant, resentful) and they stumble and fall away.

18 And the ones sown among the thorns are others who hear the Word;

19 Then the cares and anxieties of the world and distractions of the age, and the pleasure and delight and false glamour and deceitfulness of riches,

and the craving and passionate desire for other things creep in and choke and suffocate the Word, and it becomes fruitless.

Don't let the devil steal the Word (the source of your hope). Don't become offended when you are persecuted. And don't allow the cares of this life to choke out the Word that has already been planted in your heart (Mark 4). They lead only to frustration, not faith! Instead, take hold of the Word, and don't let go until you reach your goal.

Hold On!

If you've been a believer for even a short time, you know that believers still have struggles and problems. There will even be people who are going to do you wrong. You can be sure the enemy will use anything or anyone he can to distract you and take you off the course God has set for your life.

You will always have a choice to make when this happens. Will you allow yourself to be moved by the problem, or will you continue to be motivated by what God has told you (His plan, His purpose, and His promises)? The Bible tells us Nehemiah had to make that choice too. Nehemiah took hold of the plan of God and wouldn't let go until he saw it happen. Until those things he had hoped for were a reality and until he had seen the evidence, or proof, in front of him, Nehemiah wouldn't allow anyone or anything to frustrate him. He stayed in faith until the job was done.

When we are introduced to Nehemiah in scripture, he is hearing reports just brought back from Jerusalem. He is told that the wall is down and the gates have been burned; the city is a pile of rubble, and the people are scattered. He is greatly disturbed by the devastating news, so he begins to cry out to God. When he does, God begins to lay out a plan (Neh. 1).

After praying for mercy and favor for the children of Israel and for himself, Nehemiah goes to stand before King Artaxerxes. The king noticed his "sorrow of heart" and asked Nehemiah about it. (As the king's cupbearer, Nehemiah was never to be in a bad mood or have a "sad countenance.") When asked, Nehemiah took the opportunity to tell about Jerusalem's woes and his desire to go and rebuild the city. The king gave him permission as well as the resources to do the job (Neh. 2)!

Now here we see that Nehemiah has a plan from God, his hope. He also has been given the tools and the authority to do the plan. With all of that in place, you might think that the way was clear for the city to be rebuilt—it should be just a matter of time, right? Wrong! That's when all his trouble started.

The persecution began as soon as Sanballat the Horonite, Tobiah the Ammonite, and Geshem the Arab realized what he was doing. They were worried about what the rebuilding of Jerusalem would mean to them. So, they constantly tried to distract Nehemiah from finishing what he had started.

Nehemiah's adversaries were angry and began to hurl insults at the Israelites. He, however, refused to be distracted and went to the only one who could do anything about the situation: God. Nehemiah's enemies then plotted together to destroy the Israelites by bringing confusion and strife among them (Neh. 4). That didn't work either.

Still trying to thwart the plan of God (Nehemiah's hope), Sanballat and the others decided to invite Nehemiah to come and visit them. Five times they wrote a letter of invitation, and each time Nehemiah refused. No matter what they accused him of, he kept at his work on the wall. (We shouldn't come down from our God-given "wall" either.)

Sanballat and Tobiah even hired one of Nehemiah's own people to lie to him. They planned to ambush and kill him (Neh. 6). However, God had already shown Nehemiah what was going on.

Still, with each problem, Nehemiah had to make a choice. He could have become frustrated by the problems and the battles as he tried to fulfill God's vision, but he kept his hope before him—refusing to quit. With an active faith and a daily dependence upon God, Nehemiah eventually saw the wall rebuilt and the gates put back into place (Neh. 7).

I don't know about you, but I've gone through some battles too. People have done me wrong, projects have gone sour, and persecution has come through the years. Unlike Nehemiah, however, I haven't always stayed on my wall. In those times, I found myself in frustration, not in faith. Without faith, the struggles made me bitter.

Once, during a particularly difficult time, I asked the Lord what was wrong. He asked me one question in return, "Where's your hope? (What are you anticipating with pleasure? What are you confidently expecting?)"

My answer really showed where I was living: "To serve you today!" In other words, I was just looking at one 24-hour period at a time. I couldn't even see tomorrow. His question and my answer made me realize that I had lost focus; I had set my hope aside—came down off my wall—in order to fight the battles and fix the problems.

Perhaps you are where I was when God asked me, "Where's your hope?" Are you just living from one day to the next? Have you come down off your wall (God's hope and plan for your life) in order to fight the enemies that have come your way? If so, you are probably just as frustrated as I was.

Decide today to stay on that wall until everything is completed. And if you have already come down from your post for some reason, get back up there. You may have to work with one hand and keep your sword (God's Word) in the other as the Israelites did (Neh. 4), but don't allow frustration to creep in.

Keep pressing on. Refuse to just exist from day to day, trial to trial. If you stop moving forward, you will eventually lose the ground you have already taken.

In my case, I had become so frustrated that I just wasn't seeing properly. I needed God's perspective. Then, when I finally realized what was going on, I saw how my lack of hope and vision had actually spilled over on a lot of other people too. My "make it through another day" mentality had rubbed off on folks around me—they were coming and going, but not getting anywhere either. Why? Frustration will breed frustration, just as faith will breed faith; and vision will bring forth vision, just as no vision will bring forth no vision.

Frustration Speaks

Undoubtedly, both frustration and faith speak. Faith speaks the vision of God, but frustration speaks the problem. So, one of the easiest ways to check whether you are in faith is to listen to what you are continually saying.

What is consuming your time? Are you basking in the presence of God or brooding over the problem? Are you speaking what God is doing, or are you having a hard time making a confession of faith? Your answers will locate where you are—faith or frustration.

If you are living in the land of frustration, the move to faith has to happen from the inside out—starting in your spirit. For example, if you are having financial challenges, money coming in to take care of all your bills will not take you from frustration back to faith (contrary to what you might think). A new home or car won't either. Therefore, spiritually, you must get back into a place where you are no longer moved by what you see. You must learn to be motivated by the vision, not the circumstances.

Doing this will cause an amazing transformation. You won't even care if people like you or not. Your faith will keep you company, if no one else will. You won't care if you are the only one who can see God's plan. You will have something to get up for every morning.

■

The passion that burns in your heart will cause you to speak your hope for all to hear. Before long, God will use that same fire to kindle fire in others. (Be watchful though. The opposite is true as well. Words of doubt and frustration will act like water, putting out your fire.)

So, discover God's plan for you; it will bring you victory. If you're not sure what that plan is, spend some time thinking about the last thing God told you to do. Even if it was 15 years ago, find out what it was. When you remember, you'll have your starting point. You'll have a vision that you can have confidence in, and it will lead you to begin releasing your faith to go and get it.

PROVERBS 29:18
18 Where there is no vision, the people perish: but he that keepeth the law, happy is he.

I have preached this verse plenty over the years, and it always ministers to me. It especially reminds me that I must keep looking to God and His vision for me. Having seen this scripture work in my own life repeatedly, I know it will be true for anyone who puts it into practice.

Despite my frustration, God has remained faithful. In fact, I have been completely amazed at His goodness to me at times. Even when I have struggled the most—right in the middle of my "wilderness"—the Lord has continued to meet my needs supernaturally. Our local church went through three difficult years, during which I became overwhelmed by the circumstances. Yet, even then, our congregation paid off more than one-third of our church mortgage, fed folks

in our tri-state area, ministered life through the Word, and saw people saved and blessed.

Still, there I was in my frustration until God woke me up one
morning. He said, "Just think what you could do if you had a vision
again. Look what I've done with you even with your murmuring
and fussing at Me every day. Just think what I could do if you would
turn this around and hook up with Me. Why don't you let Me get
you out of frustration and back into faith where you can serve Me
and I can do what I want to do?" What a wake-up call that was!

I had lost my vision. The things of God were not motivating me.
Instead, the difficult circumstances around me were controlling me.
The circumstances were controlling my words, my actions, and my
attitudes. And my frustration affected other people and brought
with it depression and defeat. I had become like the Prophet Elijah
sitting under the juniper tree, hosting my own pity party and looking at everyone else but me. Perhaps you, too, have been there a
time or two. If so, Elijah's attitude might sound familiar. Allow me
to paraphrase First Kings 19:14:

> Look at me, God. I pray. I obey. Look! Everyone is out to get
> me, and I am the only one left doing anything. I am the only
> one doing the will of God. I don't deserve this. I need to go
> somewhere else—where people will appreciate me.

Without question, God let Elijah know (just as He let me know)
that He was still in charge. Elijah was moaning about being the only
one left to work when God announced that 7,000 others were doing
the will of God (1 Kings 19:18). That straightened up Elijah. And in

the end, his wake-up call gave the prophet a fresh perspective and renewed his purpose and vision.

Taking a closer look at Proverbs 29:18, we can quickly understand *why* Elijah was ready to sit down under a tree and die. The first part of the verse states, *"Where there is no vision, the people perish."* *Vision* can be explained simply as "the revealed Word of God." So, we won't prosper or be a success if we have no revelation of God's plan for our lives. In fact, without vision, we will want to throw in the towel just like the Prophet Elijah did.

The word *perish* means "to cast off all restraints." In other words, Elijah lost track of God's vision for his life when he began to dwell on the circumstances that surrounded him (namely, a death sentence from Queen Jezebel). In doing so, he "cast off all restraints." That means he had no direction or boundaries. He stopped walking in faith and became frustrated, which is obvious from that speech he gave to God.

Why Boundaries?

Boundaries keep us on track. Without them, we run here and there; we try this and that. In the end, however, our efforts are worthless or worse—destructive. As an example, think for a moment about what happens when water has no natural or man-made boundaries. Water just lies in a field, destroying the crop. That very water, if properly directed, can become a tremendous force for good, nourishing the crop. Furthermore, that same water can be used to make electricity if someone builds a system of dams and levees. Within boundaries, the water becomes a channel of power, a channel of blessing.

Frustration has no boundaries. It has no goals or vision. Frustration causes you to have no direction; you simply exist from day to day . . . just making it through somehow. In contrast, the revealed Word of God will begin to create, or recreate, boundaries in your life, giving you hope and direction.

An even worse situation is finding yourself "coasting" (carefree) through life. You can come to a place where you are too comfortable. One minute you feel blessed, and the next, comfortable. For instance, money is coming in, the job's going well, you have a nice home, and your family is doing fine. You don't really have anything pressing you, causing you to seek the face of the Father. Your needs are met, and even some of your desires; still, something is missing. You don't get down on your knees, praying and interceding as you used to. You don't stand out from the crowd and speak boldly for your Christ. Everything looks great, but frustration is growing inside you. Why? You've let the revelation of God's plan for your life slip away; you've allowed the enemy to come in and steal it.

Many of us are living in a land divided by a strange mix of blessing and dissatisfaction. We have allowed ourselves to lose our vision, and now we are just going through the motions of faith. Overall, we have lost the plan and purpose of God. We are living without hope, without vision. Often, we don't even anticipate God's moving. We are distracted and not accomplishing much in the Kingdom of God.

The great men and women of old had a passion that we are missing. Their passion caused them to get up before sunrise and intercede for a couple of hours. Their passion enabled them to stand up under criticism. Their passion got them through the tough times because their faith was reaching out to grab hold of the hope and vision God had given.

This one thing I know: We can't stand around waiting for passion to return. We need to actively seek the face of the Father and ask Him to burn His Word, His revelation, and His plan into our heart. We're not going to get that passion for the plan of God from watching television or reading the latest book. No, we must wait upon the Lord. He is the only One with the answers we seek.

God's Adventure of Purpose

Now that you know the truth, you have a choice—will you continue allowing your problems to consume you? Will you choose the comfortable lifestyle instead of God's adventure of purpose? Perhaps if you remember the last part of Proverbs 29:18, the decision will become easier to make: *"Where there is no vision, the people perish: but he that keepeth the law, happy is he."* If you keep God's law, His plan, you will be truly happy (blessed, fortunate, and enviable). Isn't that what we all desire?

Keeping the law requires action. The word *keep* means "to build a hedge to guard and protect."[3] When God speaks, you need to be diligent to protect that Word, for it will cause you to succeed. It is more precious than gold or riches, so keep it close to your heart. Don't let anyone steal it.

Remember, the greatest of thieves, Satan, will do everything he can to stop God's plan from coming to pass in your life. He'll do everything he can to discourage you. He'll try to convince you that you can't possibly do what God said. He'll even send people across your path who will tell you every reason it just won't work. And he won't stop there. He will attack you, your family, your business, and your church. He will attack whatever he can. His purpose is simple: to steal the Word of God from your heart—to destroy the hope you need to achieve God's plan for your life.

As I mentioned before, Satan knows the power in the Word. He knows if he can't steal that Word, or choke it out, it will begin to produce in your life. It will spring forth—*"first the blade, then the ear, after that the full corn in the ear"* (Mark 4:28). In other words, the power of the Word will produce the fullness of every promise.

Another portion of scripture promises that we will reap if we don't quit (Gal. 6:9). So, if Satan can't steal the Word or get you to give up, you will see God's Word bring forth a harvest in your life. His Word does not return void (Isa. 55:11).

To keep the Word in our hearts and away from Satan, we must respect it. That may sound strange, but it is true. Generally speaking, we protect what we respect.

Respect for the Word includes not comparing yourself and your vision with others. Why? Comparison will eventually steal your vision. How? You will become frustrated by looking at others instead of looking at God and His promises to you. Remember, you will inherit God's promises with *faith* and patience, not *frustration* (Heb. 6:12).

Respect what God has given you. Protect it; fulfill it; don't let the devil steal it! And don't be deceived. It is up to you, not someone else.

Step Toward God's Plan

We must take the necessary steps to get back to God's Word, His plan, His purpose, and His hope for us. The first step is repentance. As the Apostle Peter said, *"Repent ye therefore and be converted"* (Acts 3:19). If you repent, you should change. That means you should have a change of heart, a change of mind, and a change of direction. If you repent, you should quit going the same way you've been going. How foolish (for you or me) to believe that doing the same things would suddenly produce different results. No, there must be a change.

I'm not talking about a little shift in thought here. Repentance means that you make a 180-degree turn and head in the opposite direction. Let me give you a view of a conversation with God about the kind of turn I'm talking about. Perhaps this will help:

"Son, the first thing I want you to do is repent for letting the devil come in and steal your vision. I told you to hold on to it; so kneel down right now and confess that you allowed it to be stolen."

"But God . . . that person did me wrong."

"No, *you* lost it."

"But God . . . the situation was . . ."

"No, *you* lost it."

The point is, we are individually responsible for keeping the vision. Therefore, we must repent for stepping out of faith (no matter who or what was involved). Then, we must make the necessary change (be converted).

The next step is renewing your mind to God's ways (Rom. 12:2). Don't give your flesh the opportunity to be tired, worn out, frustrated, and irritated. Retrain yourself by speaking God's Word over you! Find scriptures to stand on and then be converted or conformed to them:

ISAIAH 50:4–5

4 The Lord God hath given me the tongue of the learned, that I should know how to speak a word in season to him that is weary: he wakeneth morning by morning, he wakeneth mine ear to hear as the learned.

5 The Lord God hath opened my ear, and I was not rebellious, neither turned away back.

Just remember that you must be diligent about guarding the Word in your heart. You didn't lose your hope overnight, so it may take a while before you can stand again. Strengthen yourself in prayer, and then take your vision and set it before you, commanding your faith to go out and make it happen.

When you turn to the Lord, focusing on Him instead of the circumstances, He promises to refresh you. After you have repented and made the necessary changes, Peter said there would be "times of refreshing" that would come from the presence of the Lord (Acts 3:19). God will energize you for the work ahead; His presence will give you the strength you need each day. (FYI: You can't get this surfing the Internet! You get this on your knees, in His presence.)

Next, you must realize that your attitude is very important to your successfully walking in faith (and staying out of frustration). Psalm 37:4 promises that you will be given the desires of your heart if you delight in the Lord. If you are delighting yourself in the Lord, then you enjoy your time with the Lord and the life He has given you. When you choose to make the most of every day and have fun doing it, you can receive the "secret petitions" of your heart (Ps. 37:4 AMPC). Start having fun again! Develop your faith (trust, confidence, reliance) in the Lord by sharing *yourself* with Him, not just your problems.

Keep Your Hope Before You

If anyone had the right to have a bad attitude and to moan and complain to God, it would have been the Apostle Paul. He was forever in a situation thast looked impossible, but we see throughout Scripture that he chose to delight in the Lord even in the midst of some of the worst circumstances. We should take our cue from this mighty man, who decided to keep his hope always before him, being faithful to fulfill the heavenly vision.

■

Faith or Frustration—Where Are You?

In Acts, chapter 16, the Apostle Paul was out fulfilling God's call on his life when everything that could go wrong did. He cast a spirit of divination out of a young woman, but her employers became angry and had Silas and him beaten and thrown in jail. You may be thinking, *Wait just one minute! They were just doing what God called them to do—they were preaching the good news of Christ.* That's right, but Paul and Silas were still placed in a dungeon with their backs bleeding and their feet in stocks.

At that moment they had a choice. How would they respond? Paul and Silas began to pray. What would be their attitude? Scripture tells us that they were delighting themselves in the Lord, praying and singing hymns of praise to God.

(You should also know that Paul and Silas had an audience that night—the prisoners were listening. The same is true today. Be watchful of what you say and do in the midst of your test and trial. Many are waiting to see how a believer will handle himself or herself when trouble comes.)

Deliverance came as these two men chose to keep their hope before them. A mighty earthquake shook the jail, the doors opened, and the chains fell off. If Paul and Silas had been praying to get out of jail, they would have escaped before the jailer could get to them. Therefore, I believe Paul was praying for God to move and work in that jail. Paul's physical pain was not controlling him, and he was not brooding over their unjust treatment. Paul was still a man of faith and hope, even in the midst of the struggle.

Paul prayed, and the power of God was released. Paul praised, and deliverance came. He didn't run from his problem; he turned it around. That's the difference between frustration and faith. That's the difference between hope and life's problems. The plan of God continued to be fulfilled even as Paul sat in prison: the jailer received salvation, and no doubt, a few prisoners were saved. Through it all, Paul kept the right attitude and saw God's salvation.

The Bible tells of another man who also found himself in trouble. Unlike Paul, Jonah had to learn the hard way. He became frustrated and ran from his part in the plan of God to save the city of Nineveh. He ended up being thrown into the sea and becoming the perfect lunch for a passing whale. (That was one big, hungry fish!)

After three days and nights, locked up in the belly of a whale with no way out, Jonah finally called on God. (How many of us have ever been pushed to the wall before we would admit our sin and ask for forgiveness?) With seaweed wrapped around his head, he repented and began to worship His Creator, *"But as for me, I will sacrifice to You with the voice of thanksgiving; I will pay that which I have vowed. Salvation and deliverance belong to the Lord!"* (Jonah 2:9 AMPC).

At that moment, Jonah chose to believe the God He served. When he did, that fish became his personal submarine. It took him all the way to Nineveh, where he fulfilled God's plan for his life.

Just like Jonah and the Apostle Paul, your senses may be bombarded every day with opportunities to quit. However, you must accept the fact that your five senses have nothing to do with living by faith. Faith believes when you can't see it. Faith trusts when you can't feel it. Faith relies on God even when you can't hear the sound of victory. Faith is confident even though you can't yet taste victory's sweetness. In short, faith knows that you have it even when you can't perceive it a real fact.

Your faith will reach out, grab your hope, and then bring it into reality, despite what is taking place around you at the time. As you walk day after day, taking step after step toward the hope God has planted in your heart, you will become stronger and more assured. Stand your ground and only consider what God has said to you. When you do, your faith will begin to speak out the vision.

Instead of frustration, experience faith in all of its creative power! Instead of frustration, watch your dreams become reality! Instead of frustration, give birth to praise!

■

A WORD TO YOU

Search your heart. Are you walking in faith consistently, or has frustration begun to creep into your life? Is your faith working for you? Are you experiencing victory? If not, why don't you be honest before the Father and just simply say: Lord, I want to obey You. I realize I need to stay in faith, giving some substance to Your plan for my life. My frustrations not getting me anywhere. I'm just spinning my wheels. Help me, Lord. I want to see Your will and Your desires come to pass.

CHAPTER

THREE

No More Faith Echoes

Y ou must decide to live and walk by faith if you are to be a successful Christian. However, it's not enough only to say that you are choosing that path. Without understanding what faith is, you will never do more than mentally assent. In other words, the faith you talk about will only exist in your head and not in your heart. Such so-called faith will be like echoes—empty words. And those empty words will produce nothing but frustration!

Unfortunately, too many Christians today fall into that category. The problems of life are swirling around them like a rising flood. Folks are up to their necks but don't know what to do. In fact, many are barely staying afloat.

Although treading water will keep you alive, it doesn't get you any closer to the shore. So, you must learn how to swim in the waters of life. For that, you are going to have to learn to use your faith.

The *King James Version* tells us *"faith is the substance of things hoped for, the evidence of things not seen"* (Heb. 11:1). However, it is not enough just to be able to quote the verse; understanding it is the key. Why? Verse 6 goes on to say, *"But without faith it is impossible to please him* [God]: *for he that cometh to God must believe that he is, and that he is a rewarder of them that diligently seek him."* Faith, then, is not an option.

What is the meaning of that word faith? Well, in the Greek it means "to rely on by an inward certainty."[1] In other words, without an inward faith, it is impossible to please God. Without reliance from an inward certainty, your actions and your words are as hollow as echoes.

Outwardly, I may have a reason to be full of frustration and fear. Outwardly, everything may be in turmoil. But one thing is sure: if I have faith, none of that will matter. I will have a certainty about me that I know God is God, and He's going to get me through it all.

Faith also means "to have confidence in."[2] Therefore, you do not have faith if you are not confident in God. If you think of it in that way, you should be able to tell quickly if you or someone else is in faith.

You can often tell by the way people act. If you see people wringing their hands, worrying and fussing all the time, they really don't believe that God is going to meet their needs (no matter what they say). Likewise, if you are making funeral arrangements, you can't possibly believe that God is going to heal you. Similarly, if your friend isn't looking at the "help wanted" sections or putting out her résumé, she doesn't believe God is going to get her a better job.

If you truly believe and have confidence that God will do what He said, your attitudes and actions would change. Confidence causes you to look up and out. Confidence causes you to make plans.

Nevertheless, true faith must be more than just an outward show. For example, I have watched people jump and dance in church, who didn't have any faith. Now, don't get me wrong. There is nothing wrong with jumping and dancing, in and of themselves, but they don't necessarily indicate faith in God.

True faith is more than just saying you know God. It is also more than just becoming excited about God. Faith is putting your trust in God, holding tightly on to Him and His promises—no matter what the situation.

Some folks may make a lot of noise, shouting in services and praying at the top of their voice, but don't have any more faith than a chair or a table does. One little scare and they run and hide. It reminds me of myself when I was a boy.

We lived up an old dirt road that ran along the side of a mountain in West Virginia. Seemed like no one would ever drive me all the way home. They would just drop me off at the bottom of the hill and expect me to walk. It was probably a quarter or half-mile long, but that wasn't the worst part. Grandma and Grandpa had told me so many ghost stories that I was scared to walk the road at night. Trees, bushes, and plenty of undergrowth covered those mountains. *Why, no telling what was hiding in there!*

Sometimes it would be as late as 11:00 p.m. when I would have to make my way home. (Your real beliefs are often uncovered when it's the darkest!) Every time, I would hug the outer edge of the road, so I wouldn't have to be near the mountainside. There was a sharp drop-off with a creek at the bottom, but I didn't care. I figured it was safer to take my chances falling because I didn't think anything could climb up the hill and get me.

That's not the only precaution I took though. I would whistle and sing as I walked along. I looked big and tough on the outside, but inside my heart was racing. And it never failed. Just as I would get to the darkest and most wooded stretch of road, I would always hear something rustling in the leaves. I'd pick up my pace. My whistling would even get a little louder, but that didn't matter.

All of my outward show did not make me braver. I was scared stiff, thinking that something was going to jump out and get me. If anything ever had, I probably would have broken all the records as I sprinted to the door in the dark. Not only that, I am sure my shoes would still have been lying in the road the next morning because I would have run right out of them.

That's just like many of us Christians today. We say the right things and even try to put on the "faith" face while we are quaking on the inside. We swear up and down that we are standing in faith—believing God for our miracle, our provision, our deliverance. The only problem is this: When something jumps out and says "Boo!" we just run a little faster or get a bit louder in our confession. Often, we are just trying to convince ourselves that we are in faith.

Are we walking in faith just because we shout or take a lap around the church? No! God is not hard-of-hearing, and He's not moved by our outward actions alone. He's looking at the hidden man of the heart.

1 SAMUEL 16:7

7 . . . For the Lord seeth not as man seeth; for man looketh on the outward appearance, but the Lord looketh on the heart.

■

1 PETER 3:4

4 But let it be the hidden man of the heart, in that which is not corruptible, even the ornament of a meek and quiet spirit, which is in the sight of God of great price.

The Lord looks straight into our hearts to see if we have confidence in Him and in His ability and desire to meet our needs. It is not enough to try to convince ourselves (and others) of our deep faith. If we have an inward confidence in Him and His Word, it will cause us to act accordingly. Trusting that God is working behind the scenes to get things done will motivate and carry you through until you see a change in your situation.

The word *faith* also means "to trust."[3] So, we could say our previous verse this way: "but without trust it is impossible to please Him." Trust is key in any relationship. For instance, a man and a woman can never move into the roles of husband and wife without trust. A child will never develop a true connection with or dependence on his parents if he does not trust them. As for me, I must be able to take you at your word if I am going to develop a relationship with you.

In the same way, you must learn to trust God. You cannot have faith without confidence, and you cannot have confidence without trust. To live by faith, you must trust that the Lord is telling the truth.

NUMBERS 23:19 (NIV)

19 God is not a man, that he should lie, nor a son of man, that he should change his mind. Does he speak and then not act? Does he promise and not fulfill?

Without faith (or without trust and confidence), you cannot please God. He is looking for someone to believe that He will do what He says. At some point down the line, you must take God at His Word.

We cannot build this inward trust and reliance based on anything natural; neither can it be based on someone else's life experience. Faith is found in your heart and is built on God's own promise that *"he is a rewarder of them that diligently seek him"* (Heb. 11:6). You must believe that He will bless and take care of you.

Perhaps you need proof of God's willingness to bless and reward. A good example would be the great patriarch Abraham. He found out firsthand what it was to be rewarded by the Lord. By the way, he is also known as the Father of Faith and is one of the first named among the heroes of faith found in the Book of Hebrews.

HEBREWS 11:8, 12

8 By faith Abraham, when he was called to go out into a place which he should after receive his inheritance, obeyed; and he went out, not knowing whither he went . . . .

12 Therefore sprang there even of one, and him as good as dead, so many as the stars of the sky in multitude, and as the sand which is by the sea shore innumerable.

When the Lord first introduced Himself to Abraham (then known as Abram), He promised to bless him and make him great (Gen. 12:2–3). In addition, the Lord declared that He was Abraham's shield and "exceeding great reward" (Gen. 15:1). Many years later, the Lord renewed His covenant with Abraham and declared Himself to be the Almighty God. After which, He commanded Abraham *"to walk before* [Him], *and be thou perfect"* (Gen. 17:1).

The Book of Galatians says we are *"Abraham's seed, and heirs according to the promise"* if we are Christ's (Gal. 3:29). Therefore, the God Who is more than enough will also reward and take care of us. We must choose, then, to believe that He is more than our sickness; He is more than our need; He is more than our hurt; He is more than our problem. All in all, He is more than anything that is facing us!

Approach God

First things first, though. Before God can meet your need, you must approach Him. Notice that Hebrews 11:6 is talking about someone who comes to God. That means He is waiting for you! However, you must approach Him in faith. Doubt and unbelief will never get you into the throne room. We can also take that one step further and say that fear and worry will keep you out of His presence, for he that comes to God must believe.

Perhaps you thought all you have to do is pray. I'm sorry, but that's not enough. You have to check *how* you are praying. Are you praying, *believing*? Or are you coming to God in fear?

The word *believe* has the same root word as *faith*.[4] So, you must have confidence in God if you are going to come to Him. You must rely on Him and trust Him if you are going to enter His throne room and be heard. He that comes to God must have a quiet confidence that the Lord will hear and answer:

1 JOHN 3:21–22

21 Beloved, if our heart condemn us not, then we have confidence towards God.

22 And whatsoever we ask, we receive of him, because we keep his commandments, and do those things that are pleasing in his sight.

1 JOHN 5:14–15

14 And this is the confidence that we have in him, that, if we ask any thing according to his will, he heareth us:

15 And if we know that he hear us, whatsoever we ask, we know that we have the petitions that we desired of him.

As a Body, we have not fully grasped this revelation. If the truth were known, we would realize that many believers today are not walking in faith. Many are not taking the Lord at His Word. They simply don't believe that God hears their prayers and will meet their need.

The Lord's desire is simple: He wants you to trust Him. He wants you to trust Him when He says, *"with His* [Jesus'] *stripes we are healed"* (Isa. 53:5; 1 Peter 2:24). He wants you to trust Him when He declares Himself your Deliverer (2 Sam. 22:2; Ps. 18:2). He wants you to have full confidence in Him when He says He *"shall supply all of your need according to his riches in glory by Christ Jesus"* (Phil. 4:19).

When you believe Him, something happens. Your faith moves God. Some may think that *need* moves Him, but that is no longer the case. The only time *need alone* moved God was when He looked down and saw humanity lost in its sin. He then sent Jesus Christ to die on the Cross and take our curse upon Himself (Gal. 3:13). Jesus came because of our need, and God loved enough to meet it (John 3:16). However, since Jesus has been raised from the dead, faith—and faith alone—moves God.

■

A WORD TO YOU

Are you confident in God? Do you *really* trust Him? When was the last time you believed God to reward you for something? When was the last time you laid out your desires before Him, instead of staying frustrated with what you have?

Why tread water when you can swim? Swimming will get you to your destination (whether it be finances, a job, healing, or peace), while treading just keeps you afloat. You haven't gotten very far on your own, so why don't you try trusting the Lord to work on your behalf?

I'm talking about having a divine, intimate relationship with Almighty God. Pull Him in as your partner in life. When you do, you can say with confidence, "Come on, devil. Throw your best shot, but you can't stop me from getting to the place God has called me to be. I am not going to spend time fussing about the problem. I am going to find out how to get God's answer."

You don't have to walk through this life alone and frustrated. When you take that step of faith, the blessings of God will begin to overtake you (Deut. 28:2,15). As you step out in faith, seeking Him, He will reward you according to Hebrews 11:6. The difference will be amazing!

God wants you to move forward, toward His ultimate plan for you. Satan, on the other hand, wants to stop you. He tries to delay you by getting you caught up in the battles he throws your way.

Decide today that you will no longer let the enemy determine your time or delay your destiny. If you will begin to walk in faith, God will decide your time and your outcome. Don't let the enemy stop you from reaching your fullest potential.

The Lord doesn't want you to spin your wheels all the days of your life, working yourself deeper and deeper into the muck and mire as you try to get yourself out of your problems. It's your choice. Are you going to keep being caught up in the daily frustrations of life, or are you going to begin to move toward God's plan for you? The key is having confidence in God.

Confession

Today, I choose to have faith in God. I will not look at the circumstances; I will look to Him instead. I'm not praying to get out of a mess; I'm praying to get a victory. I'm not speaking the Word just so I might hang on and hold out. No! I've set my goals. Now devil, you either can get out of the way or be run over; it doesn't matter to me. I'd just as soon run over you as to go around you, but either way, I am going through!

I am tired of letting the economy control how much money I can have. I am tired of letting circumstances decide how much peace I can have. I'm tired of letting situations decide how much joy I can have. I'm tired of letting people control how I am going to react.

This is what I'm going to do: I'm going to get in faith and let God decide for me. I choose to get in faith. I choose to live by faith. I choose to believe God. I choose to walk with God. Hallelujah!

FOUR

Bible Faith

In one way, faith is like a house: it must be built on a strong foundation if it is going to stand tests and storms. The foundation will keep the house steady and safe, and the foundation of faith does the same. Faith's foundation is the Word of God. You cannot build a great faith life without it. The best part about this truth is the Word of God has never and will never fail. Its success rating stands at 100 percent.

Solomon knew the power of God's promises. He saw the Lord keep His Word to his father, King David, with the completion of the Temple (Israel's house of faith) in Jerusalem. Solomon declared at its dedication, "Praise be to the Lord, who has given rest to his people Israel just as he promised. Not one word has failed of all the good promises he gave through his servant Moses" (1 Kings 8:56 *NIV*). So you see, God's own Word—His promises to the children of Israel—became the foundation for the Temple itself.

Nothing has changed. God wants to be the foundation of your personal house of faith, and He is still fulfilling His promises. Therefore, you can trust Him to do what He has said.

ISAIAH 55:8–11 (AMPC)

8   For My thoughts are not your thoughts, neither are your ways My ways, says the Lord.

9   For as the heavens are higher than the earth, so are My ways higher than your ways, and My thoughts than your thoughts.

10 For as the rain and snow come down from the heavens, and return not there again, but water the earth and make it bring forth and sprout, that it may give seed to the sower and bread to the eater,

11 So shall My word be that goes forth out of My mouth: it shall not return to Me void [without producing any effect, useless], but it shall accomplish that which I please and purpose, and it shall prosper in the thing for which I sent it."

In Hebrews 11, *The Amplified Bible* describes faith as *"the assurance," "the confirmation,"* and *"the title deed of the things we hope for, being the proof of things we do not see* (v. 1)." Legally, you need a title deed to prove your ownership of a piece of property, such as a house, a boat, or a car. If I have the deed to a house, you can stand on its front porch and threaten me all you want. It won't make any difference what you say or do because I have every legal right to grab you by the nap of the neck and throw you out into the yard. If I have the title deed, it's my house, and I am going in. In the same way, faith will give you all the assurance you will ever need in this life to take what is yours according to the Word of God.

If you build your faith—your title deed—on God's Word, it won't matter if the devil hits your body, attacks your finances, or tries to steal your peace. You can kick him off your property because your faith will be the proof of ownership you need. With that assurance, absolutely nothing can stand in your way. Build that house of faith and move in! God's Word promises that He gives everything "... we need for life and godliness through our knowledge of him" (2 Peter 1:3 NIV). So, find out what His Word says—gain the knowledge you need to take hold of your title deed. As a deed enables you to lay claim on property that belongs to you, so your faith enables you to lay claim to God's promises that belong to you.

In the natural, you may not be able to see your property, but that doesn't matter if you have the title deed. That is all the proof you need. In just the same way, your faith is the proof that you shall have whatever you are believing God for. Faith always works in the unseen realm; it is the *evidence of things not seen.* As with your title deed in the natural, the Word of God becomes your evidence and proof. Once you occupy the house, faith's job is finished. No further proof is necessary, for then you are living in your promise.

Therefore, it is important for each of us to spend the time necessary to find out what God's Word has to say about us. It is an absolute necessity that we know God's promises so that we can begin to build our houses of faith, for *"faith cometh by hearing and hearing by the word of God"* (Rom.10:17). It is only as you and I hear God's Word—His promises—concerning us that our faith will grow and be stable. Then, that same Word becomes all the evidence and proof we need until the manifestation comes.

That may seem difficult, but I challenge you to take the Lord at His Word. Rev. Kenneth E. Hagin once said something that I think will help you. He said, "God said it. I believe it. That settles it!" Since the Bible is God's Word to you, choose to believe Him. When you do, amazing things will begin to happen in your life.

FAITH OR FRUSTRATION

Acts of Trust

Your first step of faith is an act of trust. When you accept Jesus as your personal Lord and Savior, you are deciding to trust in Him for your salvation; you are choosing to believe that He truly is the Son of God who died for your sins. As you listen to God's Word to you about salvation, you begin to trust. Then, through that faith, you are saved:

ROMANS 10:17
17 Faith cometh by hearing, and hearing by the word of God.

EPHESIANS 2:8 (NIV 1984)
8 For it is by grace you have been saved, through faith—and this not from yourselves, it is the gift of God.

You'll hear folks, even some who are saved, say that they just don't have faith enough to believe. If that's the case, they have admitted one of these three things: (1) they're not in church, (2) they're in the wrong church, or (3) they're not listening when they do make it to a service. Right now, you may be shaking your head and thinking it can't be that simple. But it *is* that simple! When the Word is preached, it will produce faith. Faith will come to you as you hear the Word.

Looking in John's Gospel, you'll see the same truth in Jesus' own ministry. People began to believe that He was the Son of God (the Messiah) *as* they heard Him speak. John 8:30 confirms this, saying, *"As he spake these words many believed on him."* The crowds heard His words, faith came, and *then* they believed in Him. (We receive the same way!)

52

Now, let me show you something else. It is not enough for you just to hear the Word and believe that Jesus is the Son of God. There is much more. Jesus Himself went on to explain how believers can operate in faith:

JOHN 8:31–32

31 Then said Jesus to those Jews which believed on him, If ye continue in my word, then are ye my disciples indeed;

32 -And ye shall know the truth, and the truth shall make you free.

Even though you are a believer, there are still areas of your life that the power of God's Word has not set free. So, don't stop hearing the Word just because you get saved! That same Word that brought you out of sin into righteousness can also bring you into all the fullness of a relationship with God. By spending time in His Word and then applying it to your life, you will become a true disciple of Jesus Christ.

Many of us carried a lot of baggage into our relationship with Jesus. For example, hurts and habits were still hanging onto us. However, the Word of truth can free you from hurts and habits, and it also can bring you out of worry, frustration, and poverty—just to name a few. You can get rid of all of that just as you did the sin in your life—by faith. As you accept His Word as truth for you, that truth will set you free. (The Lord wants you to know: *"You acted in faith on My Word, and it saved you. Now stay with the Word. If you will, it will clean up the rest of you."*)

Step out in faith; trust the Lord and His Word. When you do, every area of your life will be transformed by those truths and the

One Who gave them to you. Walk in assurance with your title deed as proof to all who would question you. Take possession of all the promises the Lord has given to you in His Word.

How am I to approach God in faith? I must approach Him according to His Word. How am I going to set my goals? Set them according to the Word. How am I going to get free in my life? By acting on the Word.

So then, if the faith that God wants us to have is established on the Word of God, we can interchange *the Word of God* with *faith* and be accurate. Therefore, Hebrews 11:1 would accurately read, "Now the Word of God (faith) is the substance for things hoped for and the Word of God (faith) is the evidence of things not seen." We could also say it like this: "Now the Word of God (faith) is my title deed to those things that I'm hoping for."

Until you take possession of what rightfully belongs to you, use His Word as your deed. His Word declares what is legally yours as a child of the King. His promises are all the proof you need to move into all that He has given you. (I can't move into the house until I have a deed. I can't drive the car until I have the bill of sale. I can't possess the possession until it has been signed over to me.)

So, what do you do when the devil comes and says you are sick and you are never going to be healed? Go back to your title deed that promises health, vitality, and wholeness. As you read Matthew 8:17, Christ's declaration that He Himself took your sickness and carried your pain, you will see yourself whole and well. As you study Isaiah 53:4–5, the truth that Christ took upon

Himself the chastisement of your peace and that by His stripes you were healed becomes real to you.

God's Word will produce faith in you so that you can stand strong until you move into your house of healing. You can then take hold of your healing by faith in Jesus Christ with the Word as your title deed. This legal document says healing belongs to you.

Any challenge to your ownership that the devil brings can and should be answered. Take Christ as your example and fight your adversary with these words: It is written . . . (Matt. 4:1–11; Luke 4:1–14). It doesn't matter that you haven't seen the manifestation yet; the law of God's Word backs you up. You can tell the devil to back off. In fact, you can and should evict him from your property! Speak the truth of God's Word, and Satan will have to leave. He will no longer try to exercise "squatter's rights" on your property. When you know your rights, he has but one choice: to leave!

There's more though! Learning your rights and privileges outlined in God's Word will help you to become successful in your everyday life. The truth of God's Word will set you free (John 8:31–32 *NIV*)! Then, walking daily in the God-kind of faith discussed in Hebrews, chapter 11, will bring about a real and sustained change.

Staying Power

In John chapter 15, we discover that no one can produce God's will in his or her life without staying in the Word. Further, it is only the Word that remains in us that will produce the faith—the fruit—we need in this life. Jesus stresses over and over how important living and dwelling in Him is to bearing much (abundant) fruit (v. 5).

Looking at John 1:1, you will see that Jesus is the Word: *"In the beginning* [before all time] *was the Word (Christ), and the Word was with God, and the Word was God Himself"* (AMPC). Therefore, we must remain in Christ if we are to remain in the Word and remain in faith:

JOHN 15:4–5, 7–8 (AMPC)

4 Dwell in Me, and I will dwell in you. [Live in Me, and I will live in you.] Just as no branch can bear fruit of itself without abiding in (being vitally united to) the vine, neither can you bear fruit unless you abide in Me.

5 I am the Vine; you are the branches. Whoever lives in Me and I in him bears much (abundant) fruit. However, apart from Me [cut off from vital union with Me] you can do nothing . . . .

7 If you live in Me [abide vitally united with Me] and My words remain in you and continue to live in your hearts, ask whatever you will, and it shall be done for you.

8 When you bear (produce) much fruit, My Father is honored and glorified, and you show and prove yourselves true followers of Mine.

Three points are clear in this passage of Scripture. First, it is clear that each of us is to bear fruit. Second, each of us is to receive the answers to our prayers. Third, each of us is to glorify our Heavenly Father. This can all be accomplished if we remain in Him because the Word will produce faith in our lives, and it is by faith that we please God and inherit His promises (Heb. 6:12; 11:6).

The Lord Jesus is the Vine, and we are to be His branches. There-fore, you and I are to be production facilities for the Lord. Instead of worry, we are to produce peace. Instead of anxiety, we are to produce joy. Instead of lack, we are to produce abundance. Instead of bondage, we are to produce freedom. Instead of fear and frustra-tion, we are to produce faith. In a nutshell, we are to produce God's will in our lives, not the devil's will.

To do this we must abide in Jesus, the true Word. That means we must dwell in, live in, be intimate with, and walk in fellowship with Jesus and His written Word. You can't do this one time a week. Many of us try to feed our spirit one cold snack a week and our flesh three hot meals a day. Trying to live on the equivalent of a jam sandwich (two slices of bread jammed together with no meat on the inside) won't make you spiritually strong. If you want to produce the kind of results you see in John chapter15, you will have to do more than that.

Hear what Jesus is saying. He is promising remarkable results if and when you build a foundation in Him (and stay there). The reason is clear: When you do, you will know your legal rights; you will hold the title deed to all you need in life. Your faith will be established on the Word living inside you, and that's the only place it can grow and produce the manifestation you want. Your prayers surely will be answered when you ask in faith.

As you begin to abide in the Word and your life begins to bear much fruit, your Heavenly Father will then be honored and glorified. As His Word comes alive in your heart and begins to affect the way you live your everyday life, you will become proof of His goodness and mercy. You will *"show and prove yourselves to be true followers"* (John 15:8 AMPC).

For me, that takes my living in the Word daily. When I get up each morning and worship—walk through the house shouting the praises of God, pray in tongues as I prepare to leave for work, and then listen to a sermon that stirs my faith when I get in the car—something happens. When I keep my Bible close at hand, show up at church with expectation and a prepared heart, fellowship with others who believe in Christ and His power and then take the time to thank the Lord before I go to bed, that Word on the inside of me begins to build a vision for my life. The truth of the Word becomes alive in my heart and begins to produce faith.

It is important to point out that my faith is never stronger than the Word that is living in my heart (not my head). So, I have to get in the Word, and I have to get the Word in me. I have to dwell in it, meditate on it, and memorize it. You, and every other believer, will have to do the same.

Let me show you how to locate the level of Word living in your heart. Perhaps you want to be healed. Can you quote ten healing scriptures from the Bible right now—book, chapter, and verse? Perhaps you are believing God to make you rich and prosperous. Can you quote ten scriptures from the Bible that promise you prosperity and success? Perhaps you need the peace of God in your mind. Can you quote ten verses out of the Bible that promise peace? Sadly, for most Christians the answer to these questions is probably "No." Is it any wonder that our faith isn't working?

Whether it is healing, prosperity and success, peace, or simply living a more abundant life, it's all in His Word. So, what are you waiting for? If it isn't living within you, it can't work for you. What if a soldier waited to prepare his weapons until he saw his enemy coming over the horizon . . . ("Wait just one second! I know I have the manual for this gun somewhere! Where's the safety for this thing anyway?") That soldier would be dead before he knew what hit him. Do you want to be that soldier? If not, arm yourself with the Word of God, know your battlefield manual, and listen carefully to God's directions. Follow closely behind your Commander and Chief Jesus because He is the only One Who can lead you to victory.

Of the Heart

Sadly, many Christians have been thinking that they are in faith when they really are not. Many only mentally assent to the Word. In other words, they agree with the Word, but they really aren't in faith. You, too, can be deceived. The Bible says that if you are not a doer of the Word, you deceive yourself (James 1:22). It is not enough to think about, or even agree with, the Word; you must believe it and then *act* on it. Therefore, we must ask: *How* do we believe? *With our hearts, not our heads.*

If we believe in our hearts, then faith is of the heart. Its home is found in our spirit man, not our soul (mind, will, and emotions). For example, God's Word must become spiritual truth to us before we can have faith to be born again. However, we sometimes forget that the same principle applies to all of God's promises (not salvation only as some seem to believe). The Word must come alive in our hearts, and we must walk in it.

Faith is not what you think in your head. When your head says, "Why don't you quit?" you must answer with your heart: "I can't quit because the Word has eternal life in it, and the Word has the power to produce fruit in my life."

Tend the Seed

The Bible calls the Word of God seed (Luke 8:11). First Peter 1:23 tells us that we are *"born again, not of corruptible seed, but of incorruptible, by the word of God, which liveth and abideth forever."* Get the Word planted in you. It will begin to work in you, producing a sure harvest, if you will tend it carefully.

Each of God's promises is just like the beginning of a big oak tree, just sitting there waiting to happen. Every oak tree started as a little seed. All that tree would ever be was in that seed, but if the seed were never planted and cared for, it would never become the mature tree it was meant to be.

We need to understand something else about faith: Faith has nothing to do with our flesh. In other words, God's Word does not change or falter based on any of our daily circumstances. Either God's Word is true all the time or it's not. There is no in-between. We must believe God no matter what's going on.

Your flesh doesn't say, "I am healed!" The Word of God does, and then your Spirit-led faith agrees. Your flesh (or body) says, "I am sick. I can't make it. The doctors have confirmed it." Now, don't get mad at the doctors. They are doing their job—they are telling you what they *see*. However, faith goes beyond that which natural senses can perceive, and it says there is a power greater than that which can be seen in the natural! Remember? It is "... *the evidence of things not seen*" (Heb. 11:1). Your confirmation comes from the Word of God; therefore, you can have the assurance (faith) that you are healed and that you will get through.

Faith must be established on the Word of God because faith cannot be established on anything that can be moved. To have the kind of faith that pleases God, you must base your faith on something that will not change tomorrow. Long ago, the psalmist declared, "*For ever, O Lord, thy word is settled in heaven*" (Ps. 119:89).

Since we have already established that Jesus is the Word made flesh, then Hebrews 13:8 should further settle that God's Word does not change. You can trust it because "*Jesus Christ* [is] *the same yesterday, and to day, and for ever.*" The Word of God will still be there in two days, two years, even two hundred or two thousand years. In fact, you can read the Bible and know that it has not been altered since it was first written by inspiration thousands of years ago. It's the same Word with the same power and life of God attached to it. It will do what it says it will do.

Think about it this way. We have the same Word the apostles had. (We do, however, have a greater revelation because of their obedience.) We have the same Word the great man of faith Smith Wigglesworth used to raise people from the dead. We have the same

Word that Kathryn Kuhlman used to heal the sick. We have the same Word that Lester Sumrall used to deliver the oppressed. Their faith had to be established on the Word of God, and so does ours. The Word has not changed, and neither will the outcome—if we will only believe the Word is true.

In summary, the Word of God is your title deed to the things you can't see. It is your confirmation and assurance that everything God promised is yours. So, get up every morning and say, "I'm going to use this Word as my "real fact" until everything I'm believing for manifests in my life. I'm going to believe that God will do what He said He would do. I choose to take Him at His Word; I am going to trust Him. I am going to rely on Him with an inward certainty. My head says this is not working, my flesh says jump up and run, but my spirit says, 'The Word said it. I believe it. That settles it.' The Word is working in my life; I am building my life on the Word."

That is faith. Faith is not some crazy, fanatical something. It is simply believing God and taking him at His Word.

■

CHRIST'S WORD TO YOU

A Word of Exhortation

The following is a prophetic utterance I received once while ministering along these lines. I believe it can apply to you today.

■

Bible Faith

Spend time with Me and in My Word. Allow My Word to live and grow on the inside of you. When you do, it will be just like the seed planted that brings a harvest in season. Just as an acorn falls to the ground and then becomes a mighty tree, so will My Word when it is planted in the soil of your heart. But instead of a tree, it will produce a harvest of righteousness in your spirit and life with all of its blessings—salvation, healing, prosperity, peace, love, forgiveness . . . just to name a few.

My Word will change your life, but you have to plant it in your heart. It's not enough to carry around your Bible, or sit in church each week. My Word has to find its way into your heart where it can grow and become all that it was meant to be for you. When this happens, you can ask Me for whatever you need, and I will do it for you. Remember, you never have to talk Me into fulfilling My promises. It's My joy and delight to confirm the Word living in your heart!

MARK 16:20
20 They [Christ's disciples] went forth, and preached every where, the Lord working with them, and confirming the word with signs following.

CHAPTER

FIVE

How Faith Comes

Hebrews 11:6 boldly says, *"without faith it is impossible to please him* [God]." If that's true, then I must find out how to get faith because the Lord is, in a sense, demanding it of me. But what if I can't find it? Will I just stumble over it along the way?

I have heard people say that the Lord is not fair to demand so much of us. Many have even gone as far as to insist that it is an impossible task. That can't be so. God would be unjust to demand that I walk by faith and not give me the resources to get faith. If He did, wouldn't He be just like the employer who gives a job, but refuses his employee the resources to be successful? If so, He would be no different than the Egyptians:

EXODUS 1:11, 14

11 Therefore they did set over them taskmasters to afflict them with their burdens. . . .

14 And they made their lives bitter with hard bondage, in morter, and in brick, and in all manner of service in the field: all their service, wherein they made them serve, was with rigour.

■

FAITH OR FRUSTRATION

EXODUS 5:6–8; 10–13

6 And Pharaoh commanded the same day the taskmasters of the people, and their officers, saying,

7 Ye shall no more give the people straw to make brick, as heretofore: let them go and gather straw for themselves.

8 And the tale of the bricks, which they did make heretofore, ye shall lay upon them; ye shall not diminish ought thereof . . .

10 And the taskmasters of the people went out, and their officers, and they spake to the people, saying, Thus saith Pharaoh, I will not give you straw.

11 Go ye, get you straw where ye can find it: yet not ought of your work shall be diminished.

12 So the people were scattered abroad throughout all the land of Egypt to gather stubble instead of straw.

13 And the taskmasters hasted them, saying, Fulfil your works, your daily tasks, as when there was straw.

Everything about this story is contrary to the very nature and character of God. Remember, Hebrews 11:6 tells us that the Lord is a *rewarder* of them that diligently seek Him. A taskmaster is certainly not someone who rewards; he only demands more and more with little or no compensation. Our Father God delivered the children of Israel out of that kind of bondage. Therefore, I must believe the Lord will give me the ability and resources to walk in the faith He demands. In fact, His Word promises that He has *"dealt to every man the measure of faith"* (Rom. 12:3).

Religion often blames God. However, the Word clearly indicates that we have all been given the tools to be successful in this life. God is righteous and just.

66

■

How Faith Comes

JOB 4:17

17 Shall mortal man be more just than God? shall a man be more pure than
his maker?

ISAIAH 45:21 (AMPC)

21 . . . And there is no other God besides Me, a rigidly and uncompromis-
ingly just and righteous God and Savior; there is none besides Me . . . .

2 PETER 1:3

3 According as his divine power hath given unto us all things that pertain
unto life and godliness, through the knowledge of him that hath called us
to glory and virtue.

Do you remember that Job had to repent for questioning God and
His goodness? In the midst of his trial, he declared, *"Naked came
I out of my mother's womb, and naked shall I return thither: the
Lord gave, and the Lord hath taken away; blessed be the name of
the Lord"* (Job 1:21).

While all scripture is given by inspiration of God (2 Tim. 3:16),
I personally believe that verse contains one of the most uninspired
statements found in the entire Bible. How can I say that? God later
came along and asked, *"Will the one who contends with the Almighty
correct him? Let him who accuses God answer him"* (Job 40:2 NIV)!
Job cried out, *"I am unworthy—how can I reply to you? I put my
hand over my mouth"* (Job 40:3). He even went so far as to say, *"I
spoke of things I did not understand . . . . Therefore, I despise myself
and repent in dust and ashes"* (Job 42:3, 6). Who are we, then, to
accuse or blame God?

We should especially repent of one of our most popular accusations: *it must not have been God's will.* Such a statement reflects a lack of faith and a lack of knowledge of God's Word. Instead of blaming God, we should find out how to get over into faith so that we can walk in victory.

Faith—Three Ways

The Bible tells me three ways faith comes. First, you will receive faith by hearing the Word. Second, your faith will grow as you study God's Word. Lastly, faith comes and is strengthened by association.

Think about the first avenue to faith—hearing the Word of God. It is logical since we have already established that faith is based upon the Word. Therefore, we now know that all faith is going to come through the Word of God (Rom. 10:17).

Once you hear God's Word, thus renewing your mind to His will and desire for you, it will begin to produce faith in your heart. The Apostle Paul teaches us to *"not conform any longer to the pattern of this world, but be transformed by the renewing of our mind. Then* [we] *will be able to test and approve what God's will is—his good, pleasing and perfect will"* (Rom. 12:2 NIV). As you begin to hear God's promises, faith will begin to develop. When that happens, you will have something to stand on. This is proven each time someone hears the Gospel and decides to follow Christ:

ROMANS 10:13–15

13 For whosoever shall call upon the name of the Lord shall be saved.

14 How than shall they call on him in whom they have not believed? and

how shall they believe in him of whom they have not heard? and how shall they hear without a preacher?

15 And how shall they preach, except they be sent? as it is written, How beautiful are the feet of them that preach the gospel of peace, [the Word of God] and bring glad tidings of good things!

The story of Cornelius, the centurion, is an excellent example of how faith comes by hearing. The Apostle Peter was sent to preach the Good News of Christ to this man. When Cornelius and his household heard of Jesus, finding out that *"whoever believes in Him receives forgiveness of his sins through His name"* (Acts 10:43 NIV), they were saved and filled with the Holy Spirit. Faith had risen in their hearts as they heard how *"God [had] anointed Jesus of Nazareth with the Holy Spirit and power, and how he went around doing good and healing all who were under the power of the devil, because God was with him"* (Acts 10:38 NIV).

Cornelius was known as a devout man who feared God, but it wasn't until he had heard the Good News of Jesus Christ that he was saved. He was praying, fasting, and seeking God, but he wasn't saved. Faith came only after Peter began to tell the centurion that Jesus was the Anointed One and the prophets had given evidence to His being the Messiah.

You too must hear about the Lord before you can believe in Him. Once you do, *"'The word is near you; it is in your mouth and in your heart,' that is the word of faith we are proclaiming: That if you confess with your mouth, 'Jesus is Lord,' and believe in your heart that God raised him from the dead, you will be saved. For it is with your heart that you believe and are justified, and it is with your mouth that you confess and are saved"* (Rom. 10:8–10 NIV).

Many think only about eternal salvation when they hear the word *saved*. In the New Testament, however, saved means much more than that. It comes from the Greek word *sozo*, which includes salvation, deliverance, preservation, and safety as well as wholeness and healing. *Everything* we need in life is all wrapped up in that word.[1, 2]

Hearing the Gospel produces belief, and doing so consistently will eventually build a godly pattern of thought and develop a set of convictions based upon the Word. On the other hand, if folks believe and say, "Miracles are not for today," they likely have heard that preached and discussed. Therefore, their belief system is based upon tradition or someone's personal opinions and experiences.

A preacher can bring the Word of God to life—instilling faith in those who hear. Unfortunately, the opposite is true as well. Someone can preach something far different from Christ's Good News—planting wrong beliefs in the hearer's heart. These will then affect his or her ability to believe and have faith in a God who *always* wants to reward and bless those who serve Him.

Any enemy will eventually attack, and ours is no different. When he does, you will make decisions and take actions based upon your beliefs, whether they are right or wrong. For example, if you have been around somebody preaching it is not God's will to heal everybody, you will probably begin to think the same thing. Doubting whether it is God's will and perhaps even His ability to heal you, you will sit back and say, "I'll just put it in God's hands." Guess what? You're going to stay sick. You just sided in with the devil instead of the Word.

Maybe you have accepted the Good News of Christ's work on the Cross and have been made a new creature in Christ Jesus (2 Cor. 5:17). Perhaps someone has shared God's Word about health and healing (Isa. 53:5), and you have chosen to believe that Word. That's great, but don't stop there! God's Word also promises to bless and reward you. Are you living that way? If not, are your beliefs about prosperity and abundance based upon His promises?

I know many people who are poor and have been beaten down by life. They simply can't believe that it is God's will to prosper them. Preachers have often told them that poverty on earth will bring them greater glory once they get to heaven. If you believe that, then barely getting by becomes a badge of honor! How do I know some folks believe this? I used to sit on my grandmother's porch and listen to my family almost boast about being poor. Their belief system was wrong. They had believed a lie!

The truth of God's goodness may be difficult for some to accept. Many people have heard only about a God of judgment who is just waiting for them to make a mistake. If that's you, you need to hear the right things; you need to hear the truth of God's Word. As you hear His Good News, your belief system will begin to change and with that, your life.

The second avenue to faith is that of study. In Second Timothy, chapter 2, the Apostle Paul wrote to Timothy, saying, *"Study to shew thyself approved unto God, a workman that needeth not to be ashamed, rightly dividing the word of truth"* (v. 15). *The Amplified Bible* reads, *"Study and be eager and do your utmost to present yourself to God approved (tested by trial), a workman who has no cause to be ashamed, correctly analyzing and accurately dividing* [rightly handling and skillfully teaching] *the Word of Truth."*

Some of us believed that *study* was a curse word when we were growing up (and something to be avoided at all costs). Therefore, we might have a hard time fully understanding the Apostle Paul's command. Despite that, if we will study the Word of God, we will begin to notice that faith will grow and develop sturdy roots. (Test it out if you don't believe me!)

Study comes from the Greek word *spoudazo*, which means "to make effort, be diligent, labor."[3] Simply put, studying is more than just picking up the Bible, thumbing through, and reading a passage wherever you stop. Carrying around a verse out of the promise box and pulling it out of your pocket every now and then isn't study either. Little effort or labor is needed for either one.

I can almost hear many of you now, saying, "Whew! That's hard, preacher . . . I don't know if I can do that studying thing." I understand. I'm no different than you are about that. I have to make sure

I set time aside and discipline myself to get into the Word. I must be diligent about it. I've had to learn that I'm not studying if I hit and miss or if I just run to the Word when I have a problem or frustration. If I am going to rightly divide the Word (understand what it means) so that faith comes, I am going to have to put some effort into it.

Are you at a loss about how to study? The Prophet Isaiah shows us how. The Spirit of God prophesies (speaks) through the prophet and explains how God teaches knowledge and allows us to understand doctrine:

ISAIAH 28:9

9 Whom shall he teach knowledge? and whom shall he make to understand doctrine? them that are weaned from the milk, and drawn from the breasts.

The prophet first tells us that we must be *weaned from the milk and drawn from the breast*. When a mother weans her baby, that little one is no longer dependent upon her for food. Therefore, Isaiah is saying if you want to understand doctrine and gain more knowledge, then you are going to have to go beyond just getting your spiritual food from someone else (your preacher, for instance).

As Christians, we need to get more independent in our faith walk as we get older. That, however, does not mean that you never need a shepherd. The Bible says if you *"smite the shepherd . . . the sheep will be scattered"* (Zech 13:7; Matt 26:31; Mark 14:27 NIV). You need a pastor to preach the Word so that you can hear the truth, for by the truth we are made free (John 8:32). However, you must continue to grow, and a couple of spiritual meals a week is not going to do it for you.

Studying the Word for yourself will cause your faith to grow in a way that cannot happen if you are solely relying on a pastor or teacher. You will become spiritually stronger. Your knowledge will increase, and your ability to accurately explain the Word to others will be dramatically affected as well. Taking the time to labor over His Word will enable you to stand when life's problems arise. You won't have to wait for the pastor to speak to your situation; your faith will rise up inside you and begin to speak for itself.

The way to effectively study is lined out in Isaiah 28:10, *"For precept must be upon precept, precept upon precept; line upon line, line upon line; here a little, and there a little."* Isaiah is saying we must study each scripture in light of the entire Word of God, looking *here a little, and there a little.* In other words, be watchful that you don't just take an isolated verse or passage and build a doctrine on it.

You must study every scripture in light of all other scriptures. If Jesus is teaching about prayer in Matthew, find out what else He had to say about it in Mark, Luke, and John. If something is said about love in First Corinthians, find out if anything else is said about the subject in the rest of the New Testament. Then, look at the Old Testament in the context of our New Covenant in Christ. Remember, Christ came to fulfill the Law and the Prophets (Matt. 5:17).

I heard a fellow once who actually stopped in the middle of a verse and wouldn't read any further because the rest of the scripture did not line up with his beliefs. He just picked out what he liked and discarded the rest, I guess. Taking a verse here and a half verse there will get you into trouble every time. Rev. Kenneth E. Hagin once said that you could take half of one verse, add it to half of another verse, and make it say anything. For an extreme example, you could take Acts 1:18 and add Jesus' own command found in Luke 10:37 and say:

> Judas bought a field; there he fell headlong, his body burst open and all his intestines spilled out . . . Jesus told him, "Go and do likewise."

The point is, you need to rightly divide the Word by looking at the entirety of scripture. If you do, you will begin to get the full picture and not just a few pieces of the puzzle.

As you study, the Lord has given you another tool to use. Notice that verse 11 of Isaiah 28 says, *"for with stammering lips in another tongue will he speak to this people."* You need to get into the Word and then pray in tongues for a while. When you finish, read some more and ask the Holy Ghost to make it real to you. When you do, stop right where you are and pray in tongues some more. As you do, the Holy Ghost will begin to teach you. I guarantee that the Word will come alive to you as never before.

JOHN 14:26

26 But the Comforter, which is the Holy Ghost, whom the Father will send in my name, he shall teach you all things, and bring all things to your remembrance, whatsoever I have said unto you.

FAITH OR FRUSTRATION

JOHN 16:13

13 Howbeit when he, the Spirit of truth, is come, he will guide you into all truth: for he shall not speak of himself; but whatsoever he shall hear, that shall he speak: and he will shew you things to come.

1 CORINTHIANS 14:2

2 For he that speaketh in an unknown tongue speaketh not unto men, but unto God: for no man understandeth him; howbeit in the spirit he speaketh mysteries.

Each of these steps will cause your faith to grow. Diligently set aside time to labor over the scriptures. Remember to study line upon line and precept upon precept, instead of a hit-or-miss approach (such as opening the Bible and putting your finger on a verse). Lastly, use your gift of tongues; it will unlock mysteries. As you do these three simple things, you will become more skillful in dividing the Word. By doing so, you will see an increase in your faith in God and in His desire to reward those who follow Him.

The third avenue to faith is that of association. Although this aspect of faith is not taught as often as the other two, this principle, if applied, is one that will cause your faith to rise to another level. The Apostle Paul instructed Timothy in many aspects of his Christian walk and service, but this specifically stands out:

2 TIMOTHY 1:5 (NIV 1984)

5 I have been reminded of your sincere faith, which first lived in your grandmother Lois and in your mother Eunice and, I am persuaded, now lives in you also.

How Faith Comes

Paul first recognizes and draws attention to Timothy's own faith. He obviously noticed and admired his faith, for the apostle described it as *sincere*. Timothy must have been a godly young man whose faith stood out among others of his day. Paul is quick to qualify that faith, however. He points directly to the faith of both Timothy's grandmother and his mother, linking them to Timothy's sincere faith.

Something must have happened in that family to cause Timothy to grow strong in faith. His godly heritage had made a difference that was recognizable to those outside. Apparently, seeing how both his grandmother and mother walked in faith as Christians paved the way for his faith to develop.

I know firsthand that this biblical principle works because I learned faith through Rev. Kenneth E. Hagin. He was the reason I went to Rhema Bible Training College. I saw him on television one night and thought, *He's got what I want!* I just knew if I associated with him and his anointing that I could eventually do what he did. So, my wife and I packed up and moved to Broken Arrow, Oklahoma.

Through the years, I associated myself with him and his ministry. I watched him, listened to his tapes, studied his books, and attended every service I could. In fact, it would not be an exaggeration to say that I have spent thousands of hours listening to his messages and being in his meetings. Supporting him, I drew from what he had in abundance: *faith*. In other words, I received a portion of that faith in my own life and ministry and have been operating in it for years.

■

The Bible clearly addresses the importance of carefully choosing those with whom you spend your time. If you never have thought about this, now is the time to ask, "With whom am I associating? Who are the people I am with on a regular basis? What kind of company am I keeping? Who is mentoring me?" Your answers are very important to your future and your overall health as a believer in Christ.

Make no mistake about it, you will be influenced by those around you. They can have a positive impact like that of Lois and Eunice on Timothy, or they can destroy your Christian character and lifestyle. Actually, this principle is true whether someone is a Christian or not. You can see this every day in schools as well as in the professional arena. If you hang out with the wrong people, they will mess you up.

Those you hang out with will determine whether you have great faith or weak faith. The Apostle Paul warned the Corinthian church not to be deceived—for *"evil communications corrupt good manners"* (1 Cor. 15:33). The way that reads might not make much sense to us today, so let's look at *The Amplified Bible* version:

Do not be so deceived and misled! Evil companionships (commune, associations) corrupt and deprave good manners and morals and character.

As a believer, you may not think you would ever be swayed by those you know. However, you must always be on guard, no matter how spiritual you are. If you begin to keep company with carnal people, you will eventually be affected. For example, anyone who spends time around someone with a filthy mouth will start to talk the same way after a while. Your nature and character will become corrupted. The same is also true of anger, unbelief, sexual impurity, or lying.

Perhaps you have known people who just seemingly disappeared from church one day. The next thing you know, you hear that they have backslidden and are living in sin. You don't think that one day they just decided to no longer love God and walk away from Him, do you? No, it didn't happen that way; the process is usually a slow one. Over time, they took their eyes off Jesus and His Word. Perhaps they began to hang out with old friends down at the local bar. Perhaps they began to develop close relationships with ungodly business associates to get ahead in their profession. Gradually, they were drawn away from their first love: Christ.

The strongest person in any given association will always determine what happens. Sad to say, the sinner is often bolder than the Christian. So, you must be stronger in your faith than those you spend time with daily. If you are not, their worldly behavior will begin to affect your faith and your lifestyle. Your beliefs, your actions, and your attitudes will begin to change if you are not diligent in keeping your faith grounded in the Word:

2 CORINTHIANS 6:14

14 Be ye not unequally yoked with unbelievers: for what fellowship hath righteousness with unrighteousness? and what communion hath light with darkness?

■

FAITH OR FRUSTRATION

1 JOHN 2:15–16

15 Love not the world, neither the things that are in the world. . . .

16 For all that is in the world, the lust of the flesh, the lust of the eyes, and the pride of life, is not of the Father, but is of the world.

Let me make myself clear, though. I am not saying that you are not to befriend the lost, becoming a witness in their lives. You are to minister to them as an ambassador for Christ. However, I am saying that you should be very selective about the people you allow to mentor and advise you, for your close companions will help determine whether you will come out of life's battles victoriously.

PROVERBS 13:20

20 He that walketh with wise men shall be wise; but a companion of fools shall be destroyed.

How many of us really stop and think about the company we keep? This proverb makes it very clear that you can increase your wisdom by walking or associating with wise people. I definitely don't want to take the other option here—destroying my life.

The more I study it out, the more I see that faith can come by my spending time with those who are full of faith themselves. If that weren't true, then why would the writer of Hebrews charge his readers: *"Be not slothful, but followers or imitators of them who through faith and patience inherit the promises"* (Heb. 6:12). *The Amplified Bible* and *The Message* translation make it even clearer:

HEBREWS 6:12 (AMPC)

12 In order that you may not grow disinterested and become [spiritual] sluggards, but imitators, behaving as those who through faith (by their

80

leaning of the entire personality on God in Christ in absolute trust and confidence in His power, wisdom, and goodness), and by practice of patient endurance and waiting are [now] inheriting the promises.

HEBREWS 6:12 (MSG)

12 . . . Be like those who stay the course with committed faith and then get everything promised to them.

You can't imitate or follow someone if you're not in association with them. That term *association* indicates commitment. Building a relationship, developing an association with someone, takes effort and time. It begins with a decision, but you must "stay the course" to see the results.

Think about the boy who tags along behind his hero and dreams of one day becoming just like him. It really doesn't matter whether the hero is an athlete, a musician, a great fisherman, or (in my case) a preacher. He will follow and watch and imitate until he begins to learn and grow, developing into the same type of man for another boy to eventually follow.

You may have left childhood a long time ago, but you still need to look for people who will encourage you to grow and become something better than you are already. When you find someone who is a man or woman of faith, watch and listen. Associate with a person who is already walking in what you want—faith, health, prosperity, wisdom, gifts of the Spirit (and the list goes on).

The Apostle Paul even went so far as to offer himself as an example. He told the Church at Philippi, *"Brethren, be followers together of me, and mark them which walk so as ye have us for an ensample"* (Phil. 3:17). Strange as it may sound, everyone is following someone. Therefore, ask yourself often: Who am I following? Are they good examples of faith in operation (as Paul was)?

Imitation has been said to be the most sincere form of flattery. However, it is notable that when you follow the examples of godly men and women, *you* will receive a reward or benefit. The Apostle Paul carefully instructed the Church at Philippi to do *"those things, which ye have both have learned, and received, and heard, and seen in me,"* and then promised them that *"the God of peace shall be with you"* (Phil. 4:9).

We can see this type or relationship and the promised reward when we study the lives of Elijah and Elisha. Elijah had been instructed by the Lord to anoint Elisha to succeed him as prophet (1 Kings 19:16). So, Elijah went out, found Elisha, and then threw his cloak around him. From that point, the two were practically inseparable. Elisha was right there—learning, receiving, hearing, and seeing. He followed the Prophet Elijah until the very minute God's chariot came and caught him away. His blessing for doing so was a double portion of Elijah's anointing (1 Kings 19:19; 2 Kings 1:1–2:15).

God had anointed or given a hope and a calling to Elisha, but it was still up to him to decide to associate with one who would be an example before him. He could have stayed in the field with his oxen; he could have later grown tired of serving the prophet and returned

■

home; he even could have stayed on the other side of the Jordan with the rest of the company of prophets and allowed Elijah to cross the Jordan on his own. Elisha had to decide to be where he was supposed to be before he could fulfill what God called him to fulfill.

Just because God has put an anointing on you doesn't mean that it is just going to happen. You still have to associate yourself with the ministry in which God has chosen to mentor and raise you. You also must remember that Elijah was a man just as we are. In other words, he was a man with faults. He was up and down, in and out. That didn't matter to Elisha, though. He wasn't after the *personality* of the prophet. He was following after the anointing on the man. Like Elisha, you will have to look beyond the faults and human frailties of the person who mentors you. Instead, you must hook up with their anointing. When you do, you will be blessed.

■

A WORD TO YOU

Walking in faith is a full-time job. It is not something you can pick up one day and set down the next. It is a lifetime decision that will bring you the blessing promised in scripture. Hearing the Word, studying the Word, and making the most of your associations will most definitely cause you to become a strong man or woman of faith who will fulfill the vision God gives, but you must be consistent.

Make the choice today to live a faith-filled life. Do not settle for anything less. The Lord has given you three ways to get the faith you need to be successful and to please Him. Take stock of your relationships and make the adjustments necessary to have positive examples to follow. That includes finding a church home that will nurture you and cause you to grow in the Word and in your calling.

So, what are you waiting for? Step out and make the effort to develop your faith. God's promised blessing is waiting for you.

■

CHAPTER
SIX

Release Your Faith: Say It

Have you ever noticed that Jesus taught about the simple things of life? For example, He used fish, sheep, and wheat to reveal the truths of God's Kingdom. His illustrations were easy to understand. Unfortunately, since Christ's death, burial, and resurrection, we in the Body of Christ have often made these simple truths difficult and complicated. I believe the Lord would want us to make the principles found in His Word understandable to all who would come to listen.

Faith is but one of these kingdom principles that, to many, look impossible to achieve. Yet, faith is simple. It is our trust, alliance, and assurance in and upon the God Who *is*. If you can believe that He *is* the Lord God Almighty and that He has promised to reward anyone who seriously follows Him, then you have faith (Heb. 11:6).

However, I have found that having faith and releasing faith are two very different things. Many believe, yet they do not know how to use their faith on a day-to-day basis. It is not that hard, but if you have never been taught, or if you have been told that only certain men and women of God can possibly walk in faith (such as ministers), then it might seem impossible.

Jesus, Himself, told His disciples that they were to *"have faith in God"* (Mark 11:22). A much better translation of the original language (Greek) would be: *"Have the God-kind of faith"* (Mark 11:22). Therefore, the Lord made it perfectly clear that His disciples (that includes all believers) were to operate in the kind of faith that God has.

Jesus then went on to teach us two ways to release our faith. In fact, both are found in the same passage of Scripture (Mark 11:23–24) and are easy to remember: *say* and *pray*. That's it! It truly is that simple. The problem is, we often are looking for some deep revelation and getting stuck in the process. Two ways, and two ways only, are given for you to hook up with God and believe what He said will indeed come to pass. The first is to *say*:

MARK 11:23

23 For verily I say unto you, That whosoever shall say unto this mountain, Be thou removed, and be thou cast into the sea; and shall not doubt in his heart, but shall believe that those things which he saith shall come to pass; he shall have whatsoever he saith.

Too often, we want to talk more about the problem than about God's solution. It reminds me of a fellow who told about a testimony service held in a little church on a cold, December night. You know, many times testimony time is for just a bunch of whining and crying. It can also turn into a *"topper time."* Every person who stands tries to top the other. The first guy starts telling how bad things are, and every testimony after him gets worse and worse.

Instead of glorifying God—telling of His greatness and testifying of His saving, delivering, and healing power—the devil becomes the main topic. Doubt and unbelief take center stage, while the power of God and faith in His Word take a back seat.

That particular night, a woman stood up and asked for prayer. Her testimony was a simple one: "I just feel like I am coming down with the flu." She just sat back down in the pew, never mentioning a word about God's healing power. Everyone turned around and looked at her, and some thought, "Yup, you can see it in her eyes. She sure does look peaked." She spoke her faith—that she was sick—and the entire congregation came into agreement. Her testimony surely came to pass since the Bible says, *"According to your faith be it unto you"* (Matt. 9:29).

Our words can work either for or against us. The devil would certainly like you to give him the right to work his mischief in your life; he will use your own words against you at every opportunity. So, don't fall into the enemy's trap by confessing his plan instead of God's. Instead, stand up and stand on God's Word.

Your testimony should be one of going over, not under. For example, you should say, "My flesh is fighting me, my mind is fighting me, the devil is fighting me, but greater is He that is in me, than he that is against me (1 John 4:4). I want you to come into agreement with me for my vision to come to pass. I believe that I am catching a healing tonight from the top of my head to the tips of my toes. I'm catching it according to 1 Peter 2:24. Praise the Lord! Hallelujah. Amen."

FAITH OR FRUSTRATION

See, faith works this way: first, it goes up; then, it goes out. *Have faith in God* is "going up" faith, and *speak to your mountain* is "going out" faith (Mark 11:22–23). In other words, I go to God first to see what He wants me to do; then, I send my faith out to get it.

There is a force operating in the unseen realm. It is the same force that God used to create the universe. God released this force called faith, and He has put that same faith in every believer. We can operate in it, creating in our lives what He has said we can have. Our faith and reliance in God can be bigger than any situation (mountain) that we face. When we walk in faith by saying and believing (that He is a rewarder of those who diligently seek Him), then the Lord Almighty (El Shaddai) will take care of everything. He will bring it to me as He promised.

Our faith becomes an indicator of just how much we really want something. Are you willing to keep standing for what you need—come rain or come shine? If people can stand out in the cold, camping for two or three days just to buy a much-wanted concert ticket, then how much more should we be willing to go to our Heavenly Father and stand as long as it takes to get what we need? In the end, the question is, *Just how much do we want our victory?*

We must be diligent if we expect to receive. *Diligence* means "to be earnest, dedicated, and persistent."[1] When I am earnest, dedicated, and persistent then I won't accept no for an answer. I won't become discouraged and turn away, I won't surrender an inch, and I certainly won't get frustrated and quit!

The Power of the Tongue

Don't allow the words of your mouth to ensnare you, stopping you from reaching the finish line! Rather, let them become the path to your victory. If you don't know what to say, then speak God's Word only. Jeremiah 1:12 tells us that the Lord watches over His Word to make sure it happens. Furthermore, Isaiah 55:11 promises: *"So is my word that goes out from my mouth: It will not return to me empty, but will accomplish what I desire and achieve the purpose for which I sent it"* (NIV). Therefore, the creative power you need to change your situation is to be found in the very Word that promises you health, prosperity, peace, and victory in this life.

God Himself speaks His faith. In fact, we can see the impact of His Word every time we look at the world around us. The Lord used His faith and set the example for us to live by, for *"Through faith we understand that the worlds were framed by the word of God, so that things which are seen were not made of things which do appear"* (Heb. 11:3).

Now this particular scripture lost something in the translation. The original Greek word *rhema* was translated into English as "the word," but it actually means "the spoken word."[2] With that in mind, perhaps it will be easier to understand the importance of what we say and the creative power of our words. God took invisible words and filled them with faith.

Words are impossible to see, but you can hear them. They are, in fact, containers that will hold either faith or doubt and unbelief.

They can carry encouragement or discouragement, hope or despair. Whatever you fill your words with is what they will produce, for *"death and life are in the power of the tongue"* (Prov. 18:21).

Since faith works by the Word of God, you will have to speak the Word if you want your faith to be strong. Choose today to model yourself after God the Creator. Fill your mouth with good things—speak your faith! You can't call things as you see them. Instead, you need to call them as you want them. That's what God did.

We catch a glimpse of the Lord in operation when we look at the first Book of the Bible, Genesis. We are told in chapter 1 that *"the earth was without form, and void; and darkness was upon the face of the deep"* (v. 2). The Spirit of God was waiting for something. What was it? He was waiting for God to speak.

Until God spoke, the Holy Spirit had nothing to work with. It wasn't until "God said, *'Let there be light'"* that the power of God went into motion, *"and there was light"* (Gen. 1:3). Faith began to work. God created light out of nothing; darkness was swallowed up in light. By speaking, God had called it the way He wanted it to be, and it was.

He had *darkness*, but He said *light*. He had *waters*, but He said *dry land* (Gen. 1:6–8). His spoken faith caused His hope to take shape and become real. We want to operate as God operates, so we must speak what we are believing, and then our faith will go and get it. Again, God said what He wanted . . . not what He already had.

Often, we are being defeated because we're calling it the way it is instead of the way we want it to be. You're not framing anything if you are only saying what you already have. Many of us just reframe what we already see. To *re*-frame means "to tear apart and do it again."

Think of it this way. You just bought a house, but you can't stand the paint. Everything looks dark and dreary. How crazy would it be to go out and spend all of the time, money, and effort to repaint the inside if you bought the same color? Or perhaps your wife keeps complaining about the way the furniture is arranged. She has you move it all out into the hallway, cleans the room, and then she has you move it back into the same spots. Wouldn't you be just a little bit upset? The same thing happens when you only talk about how something is *now,* instead of how you want it to be. That is not faith, and it will not change anything. You're just wasting your time.

Perhaps Albert Einstein's famous quote will stick with you: "Insanity is doing the same thing over and over again and expecting different results." In other words, if you want a different result, you will have to do something different. Do what God does—start speaking out what you *want* to see. Make the necessary changes, and then release your faith to go after it!

Until You See a Change

Jesus, the greatest teacher who has ever lived, showed us what it meant to live by faith. He was our Lord but came to earth as a babe—by faith. Daily, He walked by faith. Later, He died by faith and was raised from the dead by faith. What's more—He now rules His Kingdom by faith. It is the law by which He operates.

In Mark 11:22–24, Jesus taught His disciples to release their faith. He used a fig tree to demonstrate the power of our words when they mirror what we believe in our hearts. Releasing faith-filled words gives substance to hope.

You can take verses 23 and 24 and practice speaking your faith. Remove the word "mountain," and put whatever you need in its place. It's a simple fill-in-the-blank. Put your particular "mountain" in the blank. This basic exercise will cause you to speak your faith, not your doubt.

For verily I say unto you, That whosoever shall say unto this (sickness), 'Be thou removed, and be thou cast into the sea;' and shall not doubt in his heart, but shall believe that those things which he saith shall come to pass; he shall be (healed).

For verily I say unto you, That whosoever shall say unto (poverty), 'Be thou removed, and be thou cast into the sea;' and shall not doubt in his heart, but shall believe that those things which he saith shall come to pass; he shall (prosper).

For verily I say unto you, That whosoever shall say unto this (turmoil), 'Be thou removed, and be thou cast into the sea;' and shall not doubt in his heart, but shall believe that those things which he saith shall come to pass; he'll have God's (peace).

Some people actually think that they are walking in faith because they won't say anything about their problem. Nothing could be further

■

from the truth! Tell the problem to go, and then replace it with faith. Speak to your mountain; don't ignore it. If you try to act as if it simply doesn't exist, you will not get victory over it.

Others say, "I don't want everyone to know that I have a problem." Well, may I alert you to something? May I just help you out? Most folks notice when you have a problem without your saying anything! Remember, mountains are easily seen.

The Lord wants you to learn how to deal with your problem through faith. Faith never hides from a fight; faith confronts it! So, acknowledge the attacks of the enemy for what they are—but don't stop there. Identify your mountains and then deal with them according to the Word. For example, you could say, "The enemy is coming against me, and I am being attacked in my body. Cancer, you have no right to be here. The Word of God says that I am healed by the stripes of Jesus. You have already been defeated and have no right to win this battle because I know that greater is He that is in me than anything coming against me. So, I speak to you, symptoms, in Jesus' Name, and I tell you to be cast into the sea. I speak to my body and call my body healed by the Word of God. I believe in my heart and now say with my mouth that I am the healed of God in Jesus' Name!" (Isa. 53:5; 1 Peter 2:24; 1 John 4:4.) Now, *that* is how you deal with it.

I've known folks who were stressed financially, but they wouldn't admit it. The bank was coming to repossess the car and the rental company had already taken the furniture, but there they were saying, "I don't have a problem. Everything is fine." They didn't realize that faith is the answer to their problem, not *denial*. Instead of this, they should have begun speaking their faith, by saying, "Debt, be gone! Lord, I thank You that You will rebuke the devourer for my sake. I believe that You are opening Your windows and pouring out a blessing so big that I don't even have room for it all, because I am obedient and I tithe. I confess and believe that all of my needs are met, because Your Word says so. I call myself prosperous, blessed, and out of debt in Jesus' Name." Then, faith would have begun to move in and start working on their behalf. The mountains would have begun to dissolve, right in front of them.

Once you begin, continue speaking your faith—and thanking the Lord for working on your behalf—until you see a change in your situation. Why? When you have taken your stand, you must realize that the battle is not over. Be assured, your adversary is not going to give up. He will try to discourage you.

The devil might quietly whisper, "It's not working . . . ," but that doesn't mean you have to listen. Remember, you believe with your heart, not your head. You can't stop the devil from talking his trash, but you can stop him from winning the battle in your life. Speak your faith, and your mountain will be removed. You have God's Word on it!

From Confession to Possession

Confession always precedes possession. You have to say it before you can have it. Jesus was very clear when He said, *"he shall have whatsoever he saith"* (Mark 11:23). In other words, you won't have it until you say it. Many people want to have it first, but even God had to say, "Light be!" while it was still dark. He said it, and then He got it.

That is the God-kind of faith. So, if I want to have the God-kind of faith, I must do the same. I'll say, "I am healed" while I'm still feeling bad. I'll declare, "I am prosperous" while I am still in debt. I'll take every opportunity to testify, "I'm free and victorious!" while I am still in bondage. You have a mouth; use it for good. Your victory depends on it.

Now, we must remember something very important as we push toward our victory. It will keep us from getting tired and giving up. We must remind ourselves that the war has already been won; we already know the outcome. The Bible says that Jesus destroyed the devil's power. In other words, Jesus has already taken care of Satan and all of his demons.

COLOSSIANS 2:15 (AMPC)

15 [God] disarmed the principalities and powers that were ranged against us and made a bold display and public example of them, in triumphing over them in Him and in it [the cross].

REVELATION 1:17–18 (AMPC)

17 . . . I am the First and the Last,

18 And the Ever-living One [I am living in the eternity of eternities]. I died, but see, I am alive forevermore; and I possess the keys of death and Hades (the realm of the dead).

Although this is true, Satan knows the power of words. So, what does he do? He tries to get us to say, "If it gets any worse . . . I just don't know how I am going to make it!" or "Oh, I thought God was going to come through for me." If he can get you talking about your problem like that, he has you cornered.

When God's Word has been revealed, the enemy comes immediately to steal it. If he can get you to quit, he has won. For instance, you're losing the battle if you find yourself saying, "Since I went to that faith seminar, everything has fallen apart. I started doing what the preacher said, speaking things, but it just got worse. I just don't know if I believe that stuff anymore. I am going to quit talking that stuff so maybe the devil will leave me alone."

Simply put, you defeated yourself. When you began to doubt God's Word and His vision for your life, you essentially took out your white flag and waved it for all to see. You turned your sword on yourself. Satan just won the only way he can—he got you to take sides (or agree) with him. This is the way it happens:

You shall have what you say,

But if you say what you have,

Then you are going to have what you say.

And if you *keep* saying what you have,

Then you are going to have what you say,

So you're going to keep saying what you have,

Which is going to cause you to have what you say . . . (and the cycle goes on).

If you are sick and you keep saying you are sick, you will have what you say—you'll just stay sick. If you're depressed and you keep saying you're depressed, you will have what you say—you'll stay depressed. Make no mistake about it, it's a cycle.

Imagine, however, what would happen if you began to say each morning:

"The Lord is my hope!"

"The Lord covers me with favor!"

"The Lord is my blesser!"

"The Lord causes me to be victorious!"

"The Lord is my defender!"

"Today, I shall rejoice and be glad in the Lord!"

(Ps. 38:15; Prov. 3:4; 8:35; Deut. 28:1–14; 1 Cor. 15:57; Ps. 59:17; 9:2.)

By speaking God's Word, you give no place for the devil in your life. So, make a daily decision to side with the Lord by saying:

"Greater is He that's in me than he who is against me."

"I'm filled with the Spirit."

"I'm a child of God!"

"I'm an overcomer."

"God's Word is working in and for me"

(1 John 4:4; Rom. 8:9; Rom. 8:16; Rev. 12:11; Ps. 119).

When you side in with God and break the cycle of defeat, you will begin to reframe your world. Then, as you continue to meditate upon God's Word—chewing on it and thinking about it throughout the day—faith will rise up in your heart and come out of your mouth. When that happens, things will start to change in your life. Remember, confession always precedes possession. You have to say it before you can get it.

Confession alone is not enough though. You must believe what you are saying. If you don't, your words are no more than empty containers. (Nothing will come of them.) So, fill your words with faith and send them out. Believe that they are working for you.

As a servant receives his orders from his employer (his master), so your faith is waiting for direction from you (Luke 7:7–10). Every believer was given the measure of faith when he became a new creature in Christ (Rom. 12:3), but that faith will sit there dormant until you speak to it. Then and only then, will it go out and complete the task given.

Don't feel bad about speaking out because faith lives to serve you. That is its purpose. Your faith loves to go and work your fields. Then, faith loves to come in and cook your meals. It also loves to clean your house and get you ready. Your faith loves to tuck you in bed, and while you're in bed, faith is out there guarding the house, just waiting for you to get up in the morning so that it can go back to work for you again. Faith doesn't care how long you make it work or how much you demand. In fact, the more you work it, the stronger it becomes and the more it accomplishes!

Believe in your words, and you will see amazing things happen in your life. For God always comes through when faith is involved. You may not be able to see it, but you can be sure it is working to bring your words to pass.

Therefore, hold on tight to what the Word says about you because you can never rise above your confession—it will determine where you go and what you do. No matter what the situation looks like, keep saying what the Word of God says. No matter what anyone says to you, keep saying the same thing. No matter how you feel, keep saying the same thing. No matter what your bank account says, keep saying the Word.

Don't waver. Once you grab hold of God's promises, *"ask in faith, nothing wavering* [differing]. *For he that wavereth is like a wave of the sea driven with the wind and tossed. For let not that man think that he shall receive anything of the Lord"* (James 1:6–7). Relax and *"let patience have her perfect work"* (James 1:4).

Avoid a Crash

Words are powerful. God framed the world by His words, and you're framing your world by your words. Think about this: Jesus reminded us in Matthew 12:34 that it is *"out of the abundance of the heart the mouth speaketh.* [For] *a good man out of the good treasure of the heart bringeth forth good things."* Therefore, whatever comes out of your mouth, positive or negative, comes from the beliefs you hold in your heart. Your words reflect who you truly are, for *"as* [a man] *thinketh in his heart, so is he"* (Prov. 23:7).

What you believe will definitely affect what you say. So, quit believing that you are not going to make it; start taking the Lord at His Word. The moment you do, your conversation will change, and that will lead to a life change.

A computer is one of the best ways to demonstrate this principle. Anyone who has ever worked with a computer knows that you get out of it exactly what has been programmed into it, and nothing more. Have you ever tried to download an attachment that someone sends, but it just won't open? Even worse is when you get the "blue screen of death." The computer is simply refusing to do anything else for you.

Something has caused your system to crash. Often, it's because of a flaw in the software program or a virus you received through your e-mail. In other words, it's "Garbage in, garbage out" as the old saying goes.

When that happens, you have to check to see what's on the hard drive (the heart of the computer). You then have to clean it, getting rid of all the unwanted junk. Lastly, you have to upgrade your system so that it can withstand any future problems.

What are you putting into the hard drive of your heart? Whatever it is will either cause you to succeed or fail . . . crash or run.

Change the Outcome

The Bible tells us about a woman who had some choices to make, just as we do. If we look at Mark, chapter 5, we will see the process

Release Your Faith: Say It

she went through and how her choices affected her. Eventually, what was in her heart governed her actions and brought about a change in her life.

When first introduced in scripture, this woman was very sick and had been for 12 years. She had an issue of blood and had been labeled as unclean by Jewish law. Although she had done every-thing that she possibly could, including spending all of her money on doctors who were unable to help her, she had grown worse. This woman was sick, defeated, and broke. Her hope was gone.

Then, she heard about Jesus. Perhaps someone told her about the Teacher who was walking from town to town. Or perhaps neighbors brought news of a family member healed. Whatever she heard, it affected her deeply, giving her a renewed sense of *hope*. Something she heard began to change the image she had of herself. Faith came, she spoke her belief, and then she moved into action:

MARK 5:27–28

27 When she had heard of Jesus, [she] came in the press behind [Him], and touched his garment.

28 For she said, If I may touch but his clothes, I shall be whole.

When her mouth began to speak what she believed, something happened. She shouldn't have been out in public, especially not in a crowd, without declaring, "Unclean! Unclean!" to all who could hear, but she pressed in to get the miracle she sought. Her new confession changed her behavior, or her actions. Then, her actions changed her outcome:

■

MARK 5:29

29 And straightway the fountain of her blood was dried up; and she felt in her body that she was healed of that plague.

This woman had heard something that developed faith in her. She spoke what she believed to be true, and then she acted upon it. She threw her hope out there for faith to go after. When she did, she got exactly what she said—she was healed. Her words of faith determined her destiny.

Jesus Himself immediately knew that "virtue had gone out of him" and turned to ask the disciples who had touched him (Mark 5:30). When all was said and done the woman came forward and told Jesus everything. His response to her tells all:

MARK 5:34

34 Daughter, thy faith has made thee whole; go in peace, and be whole of thy plague.

Her faith changed her entire circumstances. Her faith *re*-framed her world when she changed her confession from "Unclean!" to "I shall be whole!" The stories she had heard about Jesus and His promises had taken root in her heart. She began to picture herself well and whole, no longer an invalid. Strengthened with the hope of healing, her faith grew and began to act. Faith gave her the ability to fight through the crowd, fight through tradition, fight through religion, fight through everything that was confronting her. In fact, her words of faith carried her all the way to her miracle.

Paint a Picture

The same can be true for you if you come before God and allow Him to put hope in you by His Word. He will begin to paint a different picture inside you. When he does, you will start to believe differently about yourself and your situation. Hope will change your confession to one of faith, not doubt.

Faith will begin to say what God says. When that happens, you give God the right to work miracles in your life. As was the case with the woman with the issue of blood, the God-kind of faith will move you past your tradition and religion. It will push you right through the crowd, and you will end up in the presence of God. When you come into His presence, reach out by faith and touch Him. That touch will make all the difference, and you will walk away with whatever you need.

Doubt and unbelief cannot stay when God begins to change the image inside you. As a result, you will move from a place of defeat to a place of victory as you begin to speak in faith. You will become the winner you were created to be as you begin to see yourself as God sees you.

No longer will you be held back by the "I can't" mentality that, perhaps, has held you for too long. Instead, you can look at the situations that once paralyzed you with fear and say, *"I can do all things through Christ who strengthens me"* (Phil. 4:13). Once you realize that the Lord is on your side, you will gain the strength to stand and say what God says about you . . . and you'll keep saying it and keep saying it and keep saying it. And you will see results!

So, keep feeding on the Word. As your faith grows, don't keep it bottled up inside. Release it, *"for with the heart man believeth . . . and with the mouth confession is made"* (Rom. 10:10). Say to yourself, "The word is near [me]; it is in [my] mouth and in [my] heart" (Rom. 10:8 *NIV*). Just as the woman with the issue of blood kept saying within herself (within her heart), *"If I but touch the hem of His garment, I will be made whole,"* you, too, need to grab hold of the Word and keep confessing it until you see a change (Mark 5:28).

This God-kind of faith isn't the kind of faith we cooked up ourselves. In effect, God has said, "Here is the same faith that I used to create everything, and I am going to give you a measure of it. Just as it worked for Me, it will work for you." (See Romans 12:3.)

So, how are you going to turn your life around? You must quit saying what you have and start saying what God says you can have. Speak your faith, not your doubt. Speak the Word with confidence. You must remember that you are not trying to talk God into anything. Rather, the opposite is true. You speak because you have already had a conversation with God and know what His plan is. Then, you can wait with confidence (faith) for your vision to be manifested because you have already come into agreement with God's plan and purpose.

A WORD TO YOU

Speaking your faith is not a lucky charm or talisman that you grab when you are in danger (like the crosses in old vampire movies). If you are only making a "confession of faith" to make sure

Release Your Faith: Say It

something doesn't happen to you, you are living in fear (not faith). If that's the case, you can say whatever you want as long as you want, but it won't do any good. Hope and fear cannot exist together. Faith is a matter of the heart, and your real faith confession is merely the overflow of a grateful and believing heart.

■

SEVEN

Faith by Praying

Perhaps you have begun to see that all the faith in the world will not help you if it lies dormant. You must release your faith before a change will take place. If you don't release your faith, nothing will happen. You will continue to wake up in the same mess you were in the day before, becoming more and more frustrated as each day passes.

Have you ever put away money for a rainy day or something special and then forgotten about it? Most of us have. The money will do you no good sitting in your wallet or in the jar on the top shelf of your closet. You have to take it out and spend it before it will make a difference in your life.

Now let's say I have stashed one hundred dollars under the flap of my wallet. Time passes, and I forget about it. While out running errands one day that take much longer than I expected, I get hungry. I really want to stop at a restaurant, but I'm thinking my wallet is somewhat thin. Well, my hidden stash of cash won't do me a bit of good! It doesn't matter that I am carrying enough money to buy the most expensive dinner around. One hundred dollars or not, I'm going to go away hungry.

In the same way, God Himself has given each of us our own special stash of faith. Its value is far greater than one hundred dollars. However, it will be just as helpful as that long-forgotten money if we forget to take it out and use it.

The faith you need has been invested in you. Nevertheless, it won't get the job done if you don't learn how to release it and make it work for you. Without releasing your faith, your situation will not change.

As we look again at the Gospel of Mark, it becomes clear that we have a responsibility to use our faith if we want to see the mountains removed from our lives. As we saw before, Jesus told His disciples they could operate in the God-kind of faith (Mark 11:22). Thankfully, He didn't just stop there. He went on to tell them exactly how they could do it:

MARK 11:23
23 . . . Whosoever shall say unto this mountain, Be thou removed, and be thou cast into the sea; and shall not doubt in his heart, but shall believe that those things which he saith shall come to pass; he shall have whatsoever he saith.

Jesus promised His disciples that they could release faith and bring their hope into reality by speaking. Therefore, we are to speak our faith (not our doubt). The most accurate way to do this is by saying what God says in His Word about you and your situation. Just remember the key to confession is what you *really* believe in your heart. If you want a change, you can't believe one thing and say another, and you can't say one thing and really believe another.

Reading further in Mark's Gospel, you will find another way to release your faith. Christ promised that *"what things so ever ye desire, when ye pray, believe that ye receive them, and ye shall have them"* (v. 24). Therefore, the second method you can use to release your faith is prayer. Either saying or praying will get the job done. At times, you may wonder which you should do . . . *pray* or *say*. The best answer to that question is also found in Scripture:

ROMANS 8:14
14 For as many as are led by the Spirit of God, they are the sons of God.

1 JOHN 2:20
20 But ye have an unction from the Holy One, and ye know all things.

You are to be led by the Spirit of God. Sometimes God will say to speak your faith; while at others, He will tell you to pray. If God leads you to speak to your mountain, be obedient. In that case, praying about it after you have already spoken isn't necessary. The one will just counteract the other. There is no need to pray about it if you truly trust the Lord to back up His Word.

I have not always done this. In fact, not so long ago I had let this principle slip in my life. I needed someone to remind me not to nullify my confession with prayer. The Lord again used my mentor Kenneth E. Hagin. One night at Kenneth Hagin Ministries' Campmeeting, he said, "You know, if God tells you to *say* to the mountain, don't go off and *pray* about it. If you do, then you are telling God that you did not believe in your words." At

FAITH OR FRUSTRATION

that moment, the truth of his words hit me; I had been doing just that.

Right then and there, I realized that I had been putting God in a position where He could not help me. I had become as the double-minded man in the Book of James. The Lord was unable to move in my situation as I wavered back and forth between saying and praying:

JAMES 1:3–8
3 The trying of your faith worketh patience.
4 But let patience have her perfect work, that ye may be perfect and entire, wanting nothing.
5 If any of you lack wisdom, let him ask of God, that giveth to all men liberally and upbraideth not; and it shall be given him.
6 But let him ask in faith, nothing wavering. For he that wavereth is like a wave of the sea driven with the wind and tossed.
7 For let not that man think that he shall receive anything of the Lord.
8 A double minded man is unstable in all of his ways.

The devil had been playing with me, and I had fallen right into his trap. I would speak my faith, then he would come along and say, "Now, don't you need to pray that out?" I'd start thinking about the whole thing and would go back and pray about it (just to make sure). It seemed to be good, spiritual faith, but it was actually bad, carnal doubt. Having already spoken to the mountain, I didn't need to pray about it! Take it from me: Listen to the Holy Spirit, obey His voice, and then don't allow Satan to move you into doubt.

Faith-filled prayer moves mountains in your life. Think about it this way: "Whatever you ask for in prayer, believe (trust and be

110

Faith By Praying

confident) that it is granted to you, and you will get it" (Mark 11:24 AMPC). This principle is also found in First John:

1 JOHN 3:21–22

21 Beloved, if our heart condemn us not, then have we confidence toward God.

22 And whatsoever we ask, we receive of him because we keep his commandments and do those things that are pleasing in his sight.

1 JOHN 5:14–15

14 And this is the confidence that we have in him, that, if we ask any thing according to his will, he heareth us:

15 And if we know that he hear us, we know that we have the petitions that we desired of him.

Our prayer, when mixed with faith, cannot fail to bring results. So, trust and be confident that your mountain is removed the moment you pray (no matter what you see). Remember, you don't have to talk God into anything. Pray one time, believe it is yours, and count it as done. Then, only one thing is left to do: Thank Him!

Why is it necessary to thank God? Since "faith is the evidence of things not seen," it is important for you to stand your ground until your faith becomes sight (Heb. 11:1). To do that effectively, you will need to begin to thank the Lord for the answer to your prayer. Your words of thanksgiving will become an outward witness to the faith that is abiding in your heart and will eventually give substance to your hope (v. 1). In fact, always follow up your prayer with confession! It will mean the difference between failure and success:

111

HEBREWS 10:23

23 Let us hold fast the profession of our faith without wavering; (for He is faithful that promised).

The devil would enjoy nothing more than to see you give up while you are waiting to see the evidence of your prayer. Confession is your weapon to help keep you focused upon the One who has promised to meet your need. It will keep the worry, anxiety, and doubt away from your door:

PHILIPPIANS 4:6–7

6 Be careful for nothing; but in every thing, by prayer and supplication with thanksgiving let your requests be made known unto God.

7 And the peace, which passeth all understanding, shall keep your hearts and minds through Christ Jesus.

No More White Flags!

After saying all of that, I believe it is also important for us to look at what you should do if you fall down in the middle of the battle. The pressure mounts, and in a moment of frustration you throw up the white flag and scream, "I quit! This just isn't working." What happens then? Do you have to go back to the beginning? Does God make you go back and get the scripture, meditate on it, and then repray and believe God for the answer?

The answer is simple—no. The Lord just wants you to pick up right where you decided to quit. Just move back over into faith. You didn't stop anything from working; you only hindered it for a while. The devil may be whining, "You're not worthy . . . you're not worthy," but that doesn't matter. God's Word declares that "a righteous man falls seven times and rises again" (Prov. 24:16 AMPC).

No matter what your enemy does to knock you down, the Lord is fully expecting you to get up again! He is patiently waiting for you to get over your pity party, so you can move on. King David put it this way:

PSALM 37:23–24

23 The steps of a good man are ordered of the Lord: and he delighteth in his way.

24 Though he fall, he shall not be utterly cast down: for the Lord upholdeth him with his hand.

At times, you might stumble; however, that does not mean you have to go back and "renegotiate the contract" with God. That being true, don't let the devil beat you down and condemn you because you don't do everything perfectly. Just pick up where you left off.

Although faith is of the heart, you are always going to have to deal with your flesh as well as your mind. And the longer you let your flesh and your mind dictate what you believe, the longer it will take you to get to where you want to be. Therefore, it is important to understand what you should do when your head starts talking and your body acts as though it didn't hear you when you prayed and believed. (You have to be prepared, if you plan to win.)

The devil plays hardball. He will use every opportunity to cause you to doubt God's promises. First, your *mind* starts on you: "I think maybe I'd better pray and believe that I receive again; I'm just as sick as I was before." Then, your *body* adds, "Oh, I don't feel so well; I think I had better go lie down—this pain . . ." If that's not enough to knock you off track, before you know it, someone will come along just in time to tell you how bad you look.

Now, what I am about to say will be the difference between victory and failure. So, listen up! Here's what you have to do. You have to look to the Word for the encouragement you need. Renew your mind with God's Word, and then watch the situation begin to change (Rom. 12:2). In other words, meditate upon God's will for your life (His promises for you), and then speak it:

JOSHUA 1:8

8 This book of the law shall not depart out of thy mouth; but thou shalt meditate therein day and night, that thou mayest observe to do according to all that is written therein: for then thou shalt make thy way prosperous, and then thou shalt have good success.

Feed your faith, not your doubt. Whatever you feed the most is going to be the stronger. If you feed your faith, it will be stronger. How do you feed it? By meditating on the Word, speaking the Word, and praising God for the answers to your problems. Jesus told His disciples (that's you!) to pray and believe. Once you do, then speak and meditate upon God's Word until you see your manifestation. If it is healing, meditate on healing scriptures. If it is finances, meditate on prosperity scriptures. If it is deliverance, meditate on deliverance scriptures. If it is wholeness, mediate on wholeness scriptures.

You need to remember, though, that the opposite is just as true. You cannot afford to look at the circumstances, to ask your body what it feels like, or to listen to those who consistently "tell you like it is." If you do, you are not going to get the report you need to hear. Instead, ask the Lord what He thinks about your situation. Find out what He has to say and then choose to believe His report. Act upon it, and it alone, for *"the man who looks intently into the perfect law that gives freedom, and continues to do this, not forgetting what he has heard, but doing it—he will be blessed in what he does"* (James 1:25 NIV 1984).

When you are sick, speak the Word: *"With his stripes we are healed"* (Isa. 53:5, 1 Peter 2:24). *"He sent his word, and healed* [me] *and delivered* [me] *from* [my] *destructions"* (Ps. 107:20). You must say, *"Bless the Lord . . . and forget not all his benefits,"* for *"he forgiveth all thine iniquities"* and *"healeth all thy diseases"* (Ps. 103:2–3). Why? Because your faith will hook up with whatever the Word says. When it does, you'll get God's results.

A WORD TO YOU

Many of you are not winning in your faith fight right now because you are fighting the devil instead of fighting to bring forth the plan of God. You have your focus on your problem when you should have your focus on your hope, God's promise to you. It's as if you're playing a pop-up game with the devil. He pops up, and you spend all of your time trying to hammer him. But faith isn't the evidence of stopping the devil; faith is the evidence of the things of God that you hope for.

So, don't give your adversary the majority share of your time! Instead, do the following: (1) find out what God's Word has to say about your situation, (2) choose to believe that His Word is true, (3) pray your desire (not the problem), (4) confess your answer—God's promise, and (5) praise and thank Him until you see the desire of your heart come to pass.

2 CORINTHIANS 1:20 (NIV 1984)
20 For no matter how many promises God has made, they are "Yes" in Christ. And so through him the "Amen" [So be it!] is spoken by us to the glory of God."

CHAPTER
EIGHT

The Good Fight of Faith

The consistent thread of faith is woven throughout all of scripture. That thread is the principle God Himself works by, and He expects His children to do so as well. As a house needs a strong foundation to stand the storms that will come, so every believer needs faith.

We live in the present, so our faith must live and work in the here and now. We can look to the past for encouragement or to the future for hope; however, we must remember that only in the present can we change the circumstances and the life we now live. Therefore, faith must be lived out daily. It is the way we will please God and obtain His promises.

Our trust and reliance alone must be in the Lord and His desire to bless us. This must be true no matter the circumstances that surround us on any given day. For, as believers we live out our faith by trusting that He is working on our behalf. We keep our focus on Him instead of the circumstances that face us. Since *"faith is the substance of things hoped for, [and] the evidence of things not seen,"* we realize that God operates in the unseen realm (Heb. 11:1).

■

FAITH OR FRUSTRATION

Faith is of the heart, not an outward show. It is simply relying upon God no matter what it looks like and no matter what anyone else thinks or says. We can't always see Him working, but our faith is not based upon what we see; it is based upon what we believe. This belief is formed and strengthened when we hear the truth of God's Word, for *"faith cometh by hearing, and hearing by the Word"* (Rom. 10:17).

When we diligently seek the Lord, studying to show ourselves approved, our faith continues to grow as we take Him at His Word (2 Tim. 2:15). His promises give us something to hang on to when life becomes difficult. At that point, our faith steps in and believes that God will do what He has said.

Our simple trust moves God to work on our behalf because faith unlocks every principle in God's Kingdom. *Love* works through faith. *Giving* must be done in faith. *Confessions* are made in faith. A certain amount of faith is essential in everything we do, which might seem overwhelming—until you realize that the Lord has already given you all the faith you will ever need to be successful and victorious:

ROMANS 12:3

3 For I say, through the grace given unto me, to every man that is among you, not to think more highly of himself than he ought to think; but to think soberly, according as God hath dealt to every man the measure of faith.

The moment we believed in our hearts and confessed with our mouths that Jesus Christ is Lord, we were given the measure of faith. Fortunately for us, salvation is a gift we receive by grace through

118

The Good Fight of Faith

faith. It has nothing to do with us or our abilities (Eph. 2:8–9). If we would only learn and accept that the same principle applies to the rest of life as well.

That *measure of faith* makes it possible for you to get through the longest day and lead you to the rich, full, and abundant life that you have been seeking. You can live in victory because of the faith that has already been planted in you by God Himself. His deposit in you can help you overcome every obstacle, every test, and every trial. (A believer can never run out of faith—no matter what the devil says!)

The same faith that brought you to the Lord and made you His child will keep you. The same faith that blotted out your darkest sin will release the Lord's blessings in your life. The same faith that operated in the lives of the apostles is what you have been given:

2 PETER 1:1

1 . . . to them that have obtained like precious faith with us through the righteousness of God and our Savior Jesus Christ.

You and I have the same ability to live a life full of faith as the patriarchs of the Old Testament and the apostles of the New Testament. We each can obtain the same *good report* that our elders did, if we but learn to walk in the faith already provided for us in Christ (Heb. 11:2,39). Therefore, you too can come to the end of your life and be well able to say, *"I have fought a good fight, I have finished my course, I have kept the faith"* (2 Tim. 4:7).

No Believer Is Exempt

Every believer is called upon to fight the good fight of faith. Although Christ already defeated Satan, we will be forced to defend ourselves against him. We must always remember that the devil roams about as a lion, looking for those he *may* devour (1 Peter 5:8). His aim will always be to steal, kill, and destroy; but we were given faith to win every battle (John 10:10). As we trust in the Lord, nothing will be impossible (Matt. 17:20).

Our fight is never with God! Nor is it with people or circumstances. Our fight is against the devil's strategies. By enforcing Jesus' victory over the devil, we defeat his strategies (wiles) and fulfill fighting the good fight of faith.

EPHESIANS 6:10–12

10 Finally, my brethren, be strong in the Lord, and in the power of his might.

11 Put on the whole armour of God, that ye may be able to stand against the wiles of the devil.

12 For we wrestle not against flesh and blood, but against principalities, against powers, against the rulers of the darkness of this world, against spiritual wickedness in high places.

As good soldiers, we are to endure hardness. As such, we must also stay prepared (2 Tim. 2:3). We must put on the whole armor of God: the belt of truth, the breastplate of righteousness, shoes of peace and good news, the shield of faith, the helmet of salvation, and the sword of the Spirit—God's Word.

The shield of faith will stop the enemy's fiery darts that would seek to wound or kill you. However, faith is not just for protection. It also is to be used to subdue kingdoms, bring forth righteousness, and obtain God's promises (Heb. 11:33)! We are to get to the place where we are on the offensive, not just the defensive. Isn't it true that the ". . . Lord has anointed and qualified [us] to preach the Gospel of good tidings to the meek, the poor, and the afflicted; . . . to bind up and heal the brokenhearted, to proclaim liberty to the captives and the opening of the prison and of the eyes to those who are bound. To proclaim the acceptable year of the Lord [the year of His favor] . . . to comfort all who mourn" (Isa. 61:1–2 AMPC)? Yes! So, use your faith to resist the enemy and advance the Kingdom of God (Eph. 6:13; James 4:7).

You need to know this: If you will use your faith to bring forth and advance the Kingdom of God, your faith will also see to it that your needs are met. Matthew 6:33 says, *"Seek ye first the kingdom of God, and his righteousness; and all these things shall be added unto you."* So, use your faith for what it was intended—to build the Kingdom. Start being a witness for Jesus Christ; use your faith to bring healing, blessing, and prosperity to yourself and others as well.

Can you now understand why Satan will never stop trying to undermine your faith in God? When the Word of God is sown in your heart and then takes root, you become a powerful enemy. This is why it is important for us to understand the parable of the sower. Satan will try to steal the Word, scorch it with troubles and persecution, and choke it out with the cares and anxieties of the world, the deceitfulness of riches, and the lusts of the flesh. He doesn't want you to have the harvest that is promised when that same Word takes root and grows to its fullest potential. And that will happen if you will stay in God's word. Your faith will bring you the victory you seek. You will win (Mark 4:1–20)!

■

A WORD TO YOU

Although every believer has been given faith to live out this life, it won't serve you unless you do your part. For, faith, if it does not have works (deeds and actions of obedience to back it up), by itself is destitute of power (inoperative, dead) (James 2:20 AMPC). This being true, we need to use what has been given to us. Go out and receive through faith what the Lord has already made available to you. It shall certainly please Him when you do.

We have been given faith for the following:

• To worship God.

• To bring forth the Kingdom of God.

• To touch the hem of Jesus' garment.

• To be the oil and the wine poured into the wounds of hurting people.

• To overcome the devil and to defeat the attacks of the enemy.

- To rescue people out of darkness and bring them into the light of God.

- To believe God for the finances to sow into His Kingdom as well as meet our own needs.

- To boldly stand and witness to our coworkers, neighbors, friends, and family.

- To lead holy, righteous lives that will cause others to seek our Lord.

Truly, we have been given the faith of God. So, now I challenge you to use your faith to overcome life's frustrations and win your battles. The Word has set God's promises before you. Now, expect your faith to go after what you are hoping for. Your victory is just a step away!

BIBLIOGRAPHY

Chapter One

[1] Vine, W.E., Unger, Merrill F., and William White Jr. *Vine's Complete Expository Dictionary of Old and New Testament Words.* Nashville: Thomas Nelson Publishers, 1985.

Chapter Two

[1] *Webster's New Universal Unabridged Dictionary.* Random House, 1996.

[2] *Webster's New Universal Unabridged Dictionary.* Random House, 1996.

[3] Strong, James, S.T.D., LL.D. *The Exhaustive Concordance of the Bible.* Peabody, MA: Hendrickson Publishers.

Chapter Three

[1] QuikVerse (Version 6.0) [computer software]. Please note that this specific reference was taken from material found in the *Strong's Exhaustive Concordance.*

[2] QuikVerse (Version 6.0) [computer software]. Please note that this specific reference was taken from material found in the *Strong's Exhaustive Concordance* (NASV).

[3] QuikVerse (Version 6.0) [computer software]. Please note that this specific reference was taken from material found in the *Strong's Exhaustive Concordance* (NASV).

[4] Vine, W.E., Unger, Merrill F., and William White Jr. *Vine's Complete Expository Dictionary of Old and New Testament Words.* Nashville: Thomas Nelson Publishers, 1985.

Chapter Five

[1] *Webster's New Universal Unabridged Dictionary.* Random House, 1996.

[2] Vine, W.E., Unger, Merrill F., and William White Jr. *Vine's Complete Expository Dictionary of Old and New Testament Words.* Nashville: Thomas Nelson Publishers, 1985.

Prayer of Salvation
to Receive Jesus as Savior

Dear Heavenly Father,

I come to You in the Name of Jesus.

Your Word says, *"The one who comes to Me I will by no means cast out"* (John 6:37 NKJV). I know You won't cast me out. You take me in, and I thank You for that.

You said in Your Word, *"Whoever calls on the name of the Lord shall be saved"* (Rom. 10:13 NKJV). I am calling on Your Name, and I know You have saved me.

You also said, *"If you confess with your mouth the Lord Jesus and believe in your heart that God has raised Him from the dead, you will be saved. For with the heart one believes unto righteousness, and with the mouth confession is made unto salvation"* (Rom. 10:9–10 NKJV). I believe in my heart Jesus Christ is the Son of God. I believe He was raised from the dead for my justification. I confess Him as my Lord.

Because Your Word says that *"with the heart one believes unto righteousness"*—and I do believe with my heart—I have now become the righteousness of God in Christ (2 Cor. 5:21). I am now saved!

Thank You, Lord!

Signed _____

Date _____

■

AUTHOR CONTACT
INFORMATION

Rev. Darrell Huffman
P.O. Box 940
Huntington, WV 25713
www.darrellhuffman.org

"What should I do with my life?"

If you've been asking yourself this question, **RHEMA BIBLE TRAINING COLLEGE is a good place to come and find out.** RBTC will build a solid biblical foundation in you that will carry you through—wherever life takes you.

The Benefits:

Training at *the* **top Spirit-filled Bible school**

Teaching based on steadfast faith in God's Word

Unique two-year core program specially designed to **grow** you as a believer, help you **recognize the voice of God**, and equip you to **live successfully**

Optional **specialized training** in the third- and fourth-year program of your choice: Biblical Studies, Helps Ministry, Itinerant Ministry, Pastoral Ministry, Student Ministries, Worship, World Missions, and General Extended Studies

Accredited with Transworld Accrediting Commission International

Worldwide **ministry opportunities**— while you're in school

Apply today!
1-888-28-FAITH (1-888-283-2484)
rbtc.org

Rhema Word Partner Club

WORKING *together* TO REACH THE WORLD!

People. Power. Purpose.

Have you ever dropped a stone into water? Small waves rise up at the point of impact and travel in all directions. It's called a ripple effect. That's the kind of impact Christians are meant to have in this world—the kind of impact that the Rhema family is producing on the earth today.

The Rhema Word Partner Club links Christians with a shared interest in reaching people with the Gospel and the message of faith in God.

Together we are reaching across generations, cultures, and nations to spread the Good News of Jesus Christ to every corner of the earth.

To join us in reaching the world,
visit **rhema.org/wpc** or call **1-866-312-0972**.